Spirit
of
Your Soul

Insight into Life's Journey and the
Mind-Heart-Soul Connection

Peg Roberts, M.Ed.

Five Women Publishing

SPIRIT OF YOUR SOUL; *Insight into Life's Journey and the Mind-Heart-Soul Connection* by Peg Roberts, M.Ed.

ISBN 978-1-7333372-0-5 - Paperback
ISBN 978-1-7333372-1-2 - Kindle
ISBN 978-1-7333372-2-9 - Hard Cover

First Edition

Five Women Publishing

P.O. Box 1423
Newburyport, Massachusetts 01950
info@fivewomenpublishing.com
www.PegRobertsAuthor.com
Peg@PegRobertsAuthor.com

Disclaimer:
Peg Roberts is not a physician and does not dispense medical advice. This book is meant to be educational and thought provoking and is not intended as a substitute for the medical advice of physicians or other medical professionals. The reader should regularly consult a physician in matters regarding her/his physical and mental health, and particularly in respect to any symptoms that may require medical attention and diagnosis.

Cover Design: Rik Feeney, www.RickFeeney.com

Illustration and logos: Olivia Girard

Acknowledgments

Publishing my first book has been an exciting and daunting task that was made easier with the support and assistance of the following people.

This book may never have been compiled without the urging of Lee Hartman Woodbury. She has prodded and encouraged me to publish my writing for many years, so to you I say a big thank you!

My appreciation also goes to my readers Bill Hartman, Roberta Fitzsimmons and Nancy Mulligan for their time and effort in providing feedback in various forms. Thanks also to Rev. Charles Hartman for thinking enough of my writing to include it in his sermon and at two of my children's weddings.

To Rik Feeney (RickFeeney.com), your guidance, and patience with this newbie during the design and set up of the book have been invaluable. My appreciation also goes to author, Marilynn Carter, who met with me and helped me understand some of the publishing basics. Without Ping Cao, I wouldn't have a website. Thank you so much for sharing your web design expertise and advice.

For a long time, I searched for a symbol to put at the beginning of each writings and a way to translate my ideas for a logo onto paper. A huge thanks goes to Olivia Girard for using her talents to design the perfect little shell for the book and the FWP logo. I love them both.

To Jeff Walker, the *Product Launch Formula* course, coaching calls and online group support are what finally set me on the road to publishing my first book. Meeting others with dreams like mine at *PLF Live* gave me the confidence I needed to move ahead. Thank you so much!

Thanks also to family members and friends who have supported me even though they didn't know what the heck I was doing! Special thanks go to two my sons, Mike and Jeff and their wives, Jenny and Xiaoting, to my daughter, Elise and her husband Brian and to my brother Dan Girard. I love you all so much!

To my longtime friends Becky Hall, Mary O'Brien and Liz Johnston, you have no idea how much your support and enthusiasm means to me. Your excitement makes me feel special.

I know that there are a few people on the other side who are smiling, some of whom are saying "Finally!" I'm sorry that you aren't here to celebrate with me, but I know you're with me in spirit.

May you find the answers you seek and the peace you
deserve as you wend your way
through this book.

Myths are not so much legends
as they are truths that have been forgotten

Open your heart and your spirit
to the concepts contained herein

Peg

Dedication

To my grandson, Christian, who was a shining light in everyone's life. We miss your special smile and your sense of humor every day, but we know you are nearby.

TABLE OF CONTENTS

Introduction

Life has a way of taking us where we need to be at the time we need to be there. I learned this through the experiences that guided me to intuitive writing.

Although my background is in education, I found myself working in human services throughout the 1990s. At one of the agencies, I enrolled in a journaling class quite by accident. The class needed a minimum number of participants to run. I enrolled so it wouldn't be cancelled. In one of the sessions, the instructor took us through a visualization exercise and told us to write down anything that came into our heads. I'm usually not good at that sort of exercise, but I did the visualization and tried to do as she requested. As I was writing down my thoughts, I heard these words:

> *"I am the Spirit of your Soul.*
> *Listen to yourself to hear me."*

A rush of other words followed. I knew the group had finished the exercise, because I could hear them talking. I was there but not there. It was like being in two worlds at once.

That experience changed my life. At first, I was a little freaked out. How did this happen? Who was that talking to me? Then I began going into that space myself and writing down what I heard. Often when I wrote, it made no sense to me.

The words come in different ways. Sometimes, I ask a question about a topic or a situation. At other times, I physically feel the need to write, so I listen and write whatever comes to me. I also do writings for others upon request.

To begin, I go into a meditative space. When I ask a question, my conscious mind immediately expects a certain answer. I know the words are not coming from my conscious mind, because they are never what I expect to hear.

Now that I have been listening and writing for so long, I am better at gleaning the messages. There are still times when what I write makes no sense to me, but it does to others. I guess that's the way it's supposed to be.

For years, others encouraged me to publish a book. As I became more comfortable with my writing process, the thought of publishing a book began to feel more possible. Now, nearly 30 years after that journaling class, I am ready.

I believe we are constantly receiving little taps on the shoulder to help us go where we need to go. Some people respond well to the taps. Others, including me, take the long road home. The taps must become much stronger to get our attention.

I could look back with regret at all the cues I missed and wonder what my life would have been like if I had heard the taps sooner. Instead, I realize that no matter how long it takes for us to recognize our gifts, the timing is perfect.

Putting this book together has been an enjoyable process. If I had compiled it sooner, I might have done it for the wrong reason; not out of desire but out of a feeling of obligation.

More than once, I did writings about whether to publish a book. Each time, the words that came to me were different, but the message was always the same. "You will know when the time is right. Until then, let it go."

Now it all makes sense to me. I hope that some of what I have written makes sense to you, too.

The Journey

Come along on a journey to
discover yourself
Bring your heart and your soul
for they are necessary
Think not of the whole trip
but only of the first step
It is the most important and
sometimes the hardest

If you falter, do not fall back
Rest for a moment and move on
Life is made up of little successes
and failures strung in a row
We learn from all of them

Changing your life is like cleaning a house
You can give it a once over
to make it look nice
Or you can clean out all the closets
Only you will know the difference

Lines in the sand will fade
when the wind blows
While those carved into the
bark of a tree may last forever
Watch not for the outward signs,
but look inward
Make a joyful noise unto yourself
Let your music play

Your path is not hidden
It is there for you to see
Sometimes twisting and turning
Sometimes straight as an arrow
It leads you on your journey
and offers opportunities
Nothing is predetermined
The choices are yours

Turn to yourself, for you are dependable
Listen to your heart, for it is part of you
Be guided by your soul,
for it is part of the Universe

The answers have always been there
You have only to ask the questions
Get ready for the ride of your life
And know that you are never
on the journey alone

The solitude from whence we come
shapes our destiny
From the moment we are born,
there is a clanging bell within us
Sometimes loud and sometimes soft,
it leads us where we have to go
In moments of sorrow or of great joy,
In times of conflict or of peace,
it speaks to us
Reminding us of what we have to do

When we falter, it supports us
Pealing like a lighthouse on a foggy night
In our haste, it remains steady
The courses of our lives
are manifested through its song
In all things, we have choice
Those who listen reap the rewards

Consider the person who gives up
personal satisfaction for duty
The beauty of life is reduced
The sound of the bell becomes muffled

Whenever you hear the bell, heed it
For the beauty of your song depends upon it
When you are ready to move on, you will go

As precious moments tick by
Remember that there is a clock
The luxury of a leisurely exit may not exist
Work to help those around you
follow their own paths
Mark the end of this chapter
with a flourish

Solitude is needed
Become a student once more
Work to develop your talents
Seize the moment before it passes again
The plan of your life is on paper
Follow it

*J*ust as clay must be shaped,
so must be the inner workings of our minds
For it is not enough to say something
without a feeling of conviction
Chance plays a small part in what we do
Wait for the energy to seize you,
but take an active part in the process

As one wanders through the lanes of life,
magical opportunities appear
The decisions one makes, the paths
that are followed lead us to our destinies

Be not afraid to cross new bridges
or walk through new turnstiles
The world awaits us
We have only to take the steps

The roles into which we are cast,
may be painful or pleasant
Sometimes of our own making,
sometimes not
Surrounded by the tight molds of family
and time, we may feel trapped
Crying in the night and screaming by day
may let off steam, but provide no solutions

The sacrifice of soul works against us
Training ourselves not to see or hear
hinders our development
As a bird flies through the air,
so should souls take wing

If there was an 800 number for Heaven,
what would you say?
That you long for peace of mind?
That your dreams have been fulfilled?
That you just called to say hello?

When the soil is right, a seed will grow
When the time is right,
matters will resolve themselves
Conflict will melt away
Happiness will become a way of life
We are allowed to break the mold
Everyone needs wiggle room

As we sail through unchartered waters,
we must depend upon ourselves
The unknown will neither swallow us up
nor provide all the answers
Walk upon fertile ground
Create with a fertile mind
That you may find yourself
in a place of abundance

The mind plays tricks upon us now and then
We think we are headed in one direction
Then zap! We are someplace else!

The human ability to collect things
is widely known
The question is
"Why do we hang onto them?"

Consider the child
who comes into the world with nothing
With love and guidance, the child will grow,
blossom and begin to accumulate things
A favorite blanket, a special teddy bear,
a dog-eared book that must go everywhere
Each providing a sense of security

Once older, a sense of belonging
becomes important
Wearing the same clothes and
going to the same places as our friends
As adults, we collect memories,
pictures of friends and families,
the artwork of our children
Ancestral treasures and history
All become part of the fabric of life

Eventually, the pile becomes too big
The teddy bear is no longer needed
once a child feels safe being alone
Individuality thrives when a child
realizes it's ok to be different
But as adults, we often
hang on to everything

Family heirlooms become
our connection to the past
Photos remind us of special times
We start collections
We fill our attics and our cellars
But for what purpose?
Must we capture a perfect day
to know that it has happened?
Can you ever capture
the stillness of a moment?

Reverse the trend by
hanging on to what is real
The hug of a child, the beauty of a flower
The love that grows between two people
The trust of a friend
For these are what sustain us

Walk down each path as it comes
Take with you the memories that are dear
and nurture the relationships that are special
When your heart and your soul have found their home
The need for material assurances will diminish

Peg Roberts   22

In the nothingness of time, a master speaks
In those words, there is promise
Carrying water to a mountain
does not make a stream
Rise up and get on with your life
Let no threshold be too large to cross

When opportunities arise, snatch them
For there is only today
The promise of tomorrow is elusive
What has passed is already done

In many ways, we are like
small beacons set adrift in the sea
Our lights shine brightly for others to see
When the call comes,
we must be prepared to answer
It is time to live the dream,
to step up to the plate

Your name is at the top of the list
Wait not for the perfect time or place
Worry not if the water is cold
Once you are in, the water will be fine
There is great need for what you do
and great peace in the doing

Deep in your heart,
in the pit of your soul, lies a dream
It is of a rose covered cottage
A fairy land existing
in the heart of every woman
But it is a dream

Radiating from this dream
are the patterns of your life
They move you in different directions,
always seeking the dream
They sometimes lead to happiness,
sometimes sadness, sometimes despair
Still, the dream lives on,
always just out of reach

Take comfort in the happiness you've had
Hold it close, for it is a treasure
Learn from the sadness and despair
for they are tools for the future
But look now in a different direction

Of all things, be aware
Appreciate your surroundings
Enjoy each day as it comes
Wander not in the mists of regret
Let not the joy of life drain from your being

Look at the dream for what it is
and make it come true
In the fading light of day, let go of
your sorrow, for it weighs you down
In the light of a new day,
look inward and examine the dream
It is the wish for peace and harmony
that encompasses us all

See it in your mind and feel it in your heart
Let it flow forth from you
No longer hidden deep in your heart
or in the pit of your soul,
For until you do, it will remain a dream
An unattainable vision of how life could be
Believe in it, act on it, make it true for you
Be open to new truths
Open your heart to others

The rose covered cottage may take many forms
Let the love in your heart guide you
And the faith in your soul bring you peace
As the world turns and events evolve
You will find your happiness
Soul mates and loving ones
will appear if you let them
And the reality of the dream will be clear

Within the confines of our hearts
there are many chambers
Each with its own purpose
Linking them together is our life's work
For within each chamber lies a special gift

The way to all things is through the heart
Strength of character tempered
like fine steel, flexible, not rigid
Compassion for your fellow man,
genuine concern, not pity
Honesty, especially about oneself,
with oneself
Gratitude for all that has been done for you
Appreciation of the situations of others
and the sacrifices that have been made

As shadows slide across a
mountain, the landscape changes
Darkness overcomes light temporarily
So, too, with life
Situations can be overshadowed
Lives are affected and sometimes changed
Anger and discomfort must be displaced
by understanding and forgiveness

Those who have the power must take the lead
To hear the cry in the wilderness
To find justice
To seek answers
To create an environment of trust
By your actions will you be known

All shadows pass
All situations have solutions
The wisdom of others is valuable
Guidance from above can be sought
The light will appear

*F*ar below the surface of the Earth,
a truth resides
Move along, be punctual
Stay on top of your life
The most important things in life
are love, family, friends, relationships
Cast a large enough net
and you will find them all

The lungs with which you breathe require air
The surface of the earth must be sturdy
so that you may walk
On a summer evening or a crisp cool autumn
afternoon, these are the things that matter

Questions abound - always more
questions than answers, it seems
Answers are there but must be ferreted out
A moment's silence can be a lifetime
or can rush by so quickly that it is lost
In the most secret of places within you
lie the keys to your life
They are the air which feeds your soul
and the foundation upon which you walk

They are yours for the asking
Do not hesitate to take the first steps
Spend time with yourself
Listen to yourself

Hear what you have to say to you
Listen for unexpected messages
They come from your soul

Begin to ask questions
Listen quietly for answers
They will always come
Some will be loud and clear
Others may not seem to make sense
Still others will come in such a small way
that they seem to be nothing at all

Dismiss nothing
Remember everything
What seems to make no sense today
may be a revelation tomorrow
Trust yourself,
for your soul cannot deceive you

*L*ike the water that falls from a high place,
our lives tumble onward
Running after who knows what
Leading us to places we may not want to go
Keeping us from those we love
and the things we want to do
The saga goes on

In the next 10 minutes, your life will change
For having pondered these thoughts,
you are no longer the same
It may be time to make a change
To look at what you really want out of life
What parts of your life
give you pleasure and peace?
What needs to be added?

These things have been
on the back burner long enough
Find a way to incorporate them into your life
There is no time to wait
Sometimes we need a kick in the
pants to get us started

No one can be forced,
but we can strongly recommend
Others need your services
Look around you and you will see what we mean
Others from this side agree and hope you hear our words

In the spring, there will be great need
You must prepare for it
Keep yourself open and centered
It may be hard at first
as you have been avoiding this space

Practice your art that you will be ready
We will be with you every step of the way
Prepare yourself physically
as well as spiritually
As you approach the horizon,
the pictures will become more clear

Do not be afraid for there is nothing to fear
It is simply the stirrings of a new way
of approaching life
As in all things, the choice is yours

*S*mall cracks appearing on the
surface can run deep
You are wise to address them
Growing tension bursts forth
like lava from a volcano
The result can be misleading
Within us all are pockets of doubt
They are our saving grace
but can also be our stumbling block

While some parts of us
are ready to move on, others are not
Our adults make the change
Our children must follow along
In the space between change and comfort
lies discomfort and uncertainty
It is a space that cannot be avoided
Sometimes we pass through quickly
Sometimes we get stuck

In a perfect world,
everything would run smoothly
In the real world, it does not
Listen to your Self, for in your deepest
thoughts, you will find solutions.
The champagne that follows
the event may taste bitter
As it is not a victory, but a change
What you are doing is of necessity, not desire

Peg Roberts   **32**

When one phase of life ends, another begins
The mistake is not in ending
but in failing to begin
For every loss, there is a gain
For every tear of sadness,
there is a spark of joy
However disjointed the process may feel,
your core will pull you together

Relationships build slowly
and they end slowly over time
The page may turn slowly,
but it has already begun to move
Don't fight the feelings
Work them through
You will not shatter; nor will you fall
Your journey will not be long,
if you keep moving

When the moon rises, when babies sleep
The light from a lone star shines upon you
It brings you peace and contentment
It can shine through clouds in the sky
but not clouds in your heart
Then it is a rainy day inside

The lesson to be learned,
the path to be walked are clearly marked
for those who are ready to see
If you are confused or uncertain,
stand back a little
Try to get on the outside
Look at a broader perspective
Let your soul cover new territory
and come back to this later
Open your heart to new perspectives

When stymied, ask for help
The light will always be there
shining upon you
When you are alone,
it can make you feel whole
If you are sad, it can comfort you
It can soften your rage or deepen your love

The way to the soul is through the heart
It is a journey made many times for many reasons
Is it time to go again?

As you pick up the pieces
of your life, look them over
Is there anything missing?
Do you have everything?

If you feel a lack,
stop and ask yourself where you are going
Look to see where you have been
You may rewrite the same story
a hundred times, a thousand times
Until you get it right
Until you are ready to see

Up to that point, the cloud in your heart remains,
causing a fog in your brain
Dampening the light from your star
Do not despair, as you will get there
when you are ready

Each step you take brings you closer
Each question you ask will receive an answer
Each time you ask for help, it will be given
The mumbo jumbo will begin to disappear
The fog will lift, and the clouds will dissipate
It has happened before
You must be patient
It will happen again

Your position belies where you are
Your physical presence is in one place
Your spiritual in another -
a little out of balance overall
In the quiet places of your mind,
listen for a song
Adopt it as your own
Lay claim to its words
Absorb the melody into your being

Quietness is key
Prayer will help
There may be too many things going on
Make time for yourself
Take care of old business
for it weighs you down
Communicate with yourself – a lot

It takes energy
to include everyone in your life
Invite them in, but do not take them on
You are a small piece of their lives
Make them a small piece of yours
The important thing is that you are there

You are looking for answers
that may not be there yet
Life can be unsettling
Lean into it

Do not pull away
for the answers will come
The realm of today is an in-between
space fraught with uncertainties
You will pass through it unscathed,
but your consciousness will change

The cover of the book will remain the same,
but the text will be different
Resistance will only delay what is to be
Commitment to a different way
is sometimes difficult
Stand far enough back to see
the whole picture
You are moving even though
you think you're standing still
Rest for now before your journey continues

Clearing a path is not always easy
When debris is in the way, one can
shove it to one side or go through it
Each must decide what to do
Is it sometimes better to
sweep it all away for a fresh start?
Or is it better to look at each piece
to decide what is worth keeping?

Reflect upon your options
Each leads in a different direction
Each accomplishes different ends
The course you choose may be
straight with no detours
It may also wind
like a river seeking the sea

You will learn much about yourself
as you travel on
Each lesson will help you
with what is to come
We ache for what we do not have
and do not see what is already there

Look about you
Be thankful for those who love you
Be patient with those who press your buttons
For they are a reflection of you
Remove yourself from unpleasant situations

That you may more clearly
see the big picture
Be clear with yourself
and communicate clearly with others
For in silence, we can be our own worst enemy

Relationships must be maintained
They are like a fire
We are only warmed by them,
If we stay close by
If we do not stoke and feed them
They will falter and the flame will die
If we hover over them, we will get burned

In the dead of winter and
the dark of night, they are there
Respect and nurture them
But do not be afraid of them
For they are what give meaning to our lives
Be as open as you can, for you will receive
great blessings from them

*T*here's more to life than simply
knowing where you are headed
The grandeur is in the "hows" and "whys"
Quality is in the "ways"
Crosscutting winds swirl
snow in all directions
We can feel lost
even though we know where we are

The paths we travel are fraught with uncertainties
Our moves, though mapped well in our heads,
are sometimes hard to carry out
Wait no longer for the right answer or the perfect time
For in reality, perfection does not exist

Think more in terms of timing
A rising tide floats all boats
You can't do much if you're stuck in the sand
Or can you?
Perhaps it is time to build sandcastles

The longer we wait, the harder it is to move
The cornerstone of our lives has been laid
It is ok to start building
As your life rises before you, you must
hold yourself sacred, for you are its creator
One soul of many
Making its way in this world
Trying to do what is best

Let the substance of which you are made
rise to the surface, that you may feel whole
Listen to yourself,
that you may hear what you have to say
Believe what you hear
Take it to heart as you continue your journey

*Th*e fewer words, the better
Your sadness and anger are understandable
Feelings that must be validated
Beyond that, there is much to do
Your presence is awaited in another world

Worry not how you will survive
All things have led you to this place
The feelings will pass,
leaving only opportunity
Have faith in those who love you
and are there for you
Take advantage of their offers

Respect yourself enough
to assess your talents
Work with those who believe in you
Waste no time on those who do not care
Look at your barriers
They are holding you back.

In the end, there is only the light
How far into it you walk is up to you
Once the barriers are gone, the river will flow
Hold back no more
Find the help you need

You have already started down the path
But it is parallel to your current life
Think about branching off,
as scary as that may seem
You have read enough books
The next step is action
Fear of failure or success, loss of income
and independence are legitimate concerns

Look at each one
Make a plan – best- and worst-case scenarios
Your answer will come
long before your plans run out
Each ending is a new beginning
Let it happen
Let it unfold
Be your own wonderful self
I am with you
Enjoy the peace

The material goods of this world
are not the focus
They stand in your way,
keeping you from your business
Poverty, while not always pleasant,
is not the end of the world
It has its place, as do all places in life

To be fruitful, you must do your work,
the work that you love
When inviting someone in for tea
Make a special place for them –
comfortable and inviting
Ask them to sit and chat for a while
Treat them like royalty

When they leave, analyze the results
Was it enjoyable?
Were they comfortable?
Would they come again?

Now apply this to your life
Find your passion and invite it in
Let go of notions that hinder you
Meditate to remove barriers
Let your heart soar,
for it should not be held back
Keep your goals in front of you at all times
Check in with yourself regularly

Where are you in relation to your goals?
Are you having fun? Is it still a treat?

The problem of focus is internal
The best idea, hampered by doubts,
will go nowhere
The greatest talent, if unused,
will never shine
A vote of confidence in yourself
A slap on your own back is important

Set attainable goals
In your moments of hesitation,
release all doubts
Stay connected with the world,
for isolation does not suit you

The colleagues with whom you
work will be supportive
Friends and family will be there for you
Other connections will appear
Other opportunities will arise
Keep your goals in front of you

Reluctance is the only thing
holding you back
Release the reluctance to succeed
Release the reluctance to face failure
Banish the reluctance to believe in yourself
Each day that you progress is successful
For success may sometimes be
as simple as a smile

What is seen by the world as failure
is just another opportunity to learn
Our belief in ourselves is bolstered
by our ability to recognize our successes
and learn from our failures

The price we pay to reach our goals
must be in keeping with our Spirit
Our comfort level must always be high
We must treat our Selves like royalty
And we must always want
to come back again for tea

The Struggle

The joys in life do not always come easily
Important moments must be clung to
as their memory must last a lifetime
Frost on windowpanes disappears
as the day warms
Yet we know that it has been there
and that it will come again
Like a river that flows to the sea
Life begins at the source
and travels into the great beyond

Sometimes we wonder how we can go on
The pain is so great
and the world seems so large
In times of peaceful contemplation,
we connect with our innermost being
and realize how small the planet is

Torn apart by inner conflict, we seek answers
for ourselves and those we love;
Only to realize that
we cannot be all things to all people
The art of compromise
is useful for the external
But we must never compromise our soul
For it is our source, our well-spring
The place from which our essence comes

Ask a question of yourself
and the answer will come
The fogginess inside your head will lift
as clouds from a mountain top
Your whole being will work to find the answer,
for it has no choice

The answer may be in the trickle
of a brook or the buzz of a bee
You may hear it in the passing comment
of a friend or the dialogue of a play
You may read it in a magazine
or in the writings of a child

But have no fear, the answers will come,
if you are open to them
For are we not vessels of our God?
Do we not have access to our own Truths?

Elusive as they may seem to be,
they are there waiting for you
Your access to knowledge and truth
is limited only by the questions you ask
Ask wisely or with abandon
It matters only that you ask and
that you be willing to hear the answers

Be a child of the Universe
Hear what is being said to you
Struggle not to find answers
Let them come

Peg Roberts   **50**

A short meditation may free up more information
than hours of research in a library
For life's directions are not prepackaged
The harder you look, the more obscure the signs

The solution is to surrender to yourself
Listen to the messages that are inscribed on your soul
In them are your lost peace and tranquility,
your insight and inspiration
Look inward to truly see and hear with your
heart that you may be fulfilled

West winds blow softly through a summer field
Rise up over the mountains and down into the valleys
They bring with them hope for the future
They soothe the brow of one who toils hard
Lean into the winds that they may refresh you
Release your burdens that they may be blown away

What will remain are the issues that are important
Deal with them; take responsibility for what is yours
Develop a plan
Realize that solutions take time
Enlist the help of others when appropriate
Pray for the strength to keep yourself on track
These things are necessary to move ahead

When you go in circles over the same
territory again and again,
You create ruts that can become very deep
Climbing out and moving on
becomes more and more difficult
Energy is sapped
Health can suffer

The simple pleasures of life are missed
They are the most important things
You know you are ready
So, light the fire that is needed
and get the show on the road

*O*ccasionally, each of us
wanders down a lonely path
as we struggle with different
aspects of our lives
It's not the end of the world,
although it may seem that way
The landscape is bleak
We feel alone, even when we are not

The power we speak of is the energy of life
When it flows from you, you are weakened
You may feel lost or helpless, like nothing matters
To ebb that flow, look at the cause
Take the time to examine your life

Sometimes we get sucked into a space
by others who are already there
Sometimes it is of our own making
Sometimes circumstances lead us there
How we get there and
how we get out are enmeshed

The ice beneath the snow can be slippery
Make your way carefully and thoughtfully
Be thorough in your examination,
for the energy of life is precious
Go beneath the surface
as you look for answers

Realize that no one can take
your energy from you
That you are letting it go
When we get stuck in one place
or allow ourselves to stay in a bad space
We must reverse the trend

Meditate
Count your blessings
Look at the other side of the coin
Consider your options; pray
Draw in new energy from above

Ponder what part of you allows this to happen
Is it a wounded child? An angry adult?
Perhaps you just need a good cry
to release pent up emotions
Or a major lifestyle change may be in order

Get in touch with yourself
For when you do, the answers will come
They may appear subtly like a fresh spring breeze
or flash before you like lightening
They will resonate to the core of your being

Listen to yourself,
for wisdom comes from within
Have faith in yourself,
for you can overcome any strife
The road may be long
The trip may be rough
But you will triumph in the end

When we fight ourselves, we cannot win
The conflict becomes intolerable
Health, relationships, quality of life suffer
Pain, not felt, is stored in every part of the body
like a scream waiting to let loose
Circumstances, hidden from those we love,
create internal pressure

We struggle against ourselves
Sometimes to protect ourselves
Sometimes to protect others
Whatever the reason, the price is too high
Internal strife keeps us from our work
Separating us from our feelings, our inner beings
Putting up barriers that can come between us
and just about everything else

We are so clever that we hide them
Allowing them to exist,
even without our knowledge
They weigh us down,
draining energy from our bodies
Manifesting themselves through fatigue
Materializing as aches and pains

We work so hard to maintain the status quo
Would it not be better to look inside
and face the issues hanging over our heads?
They hamper our progress in every way imaginable

They curb our freedom
and keep us from singing our song
Remember that you are dealing with yourself,
not a stranger

If the task is overwhelming, seek help
Pray to the One who guides you
Tell yourself that you need to talk
Confer with professionals
They can be of great assistance

Leave no stone unturned
The price is hard work
The gift is peace of mind
Proceed slowly but without delay
The goal is to be whole
Put as much effort into you
as you do everything else
You will be pleased with the result

The question of barriers is an interesting one
A barrier to one person is a challenge to another
Motivation plays into it, too
If the barrier blocked the way to food,
you would be very motivated
to go around or through it
Perhaps there needs to be
more dedication to the cause
Perhaps the question is "What is keeping you
from committing to the cause?"

The threshold over which we step when
we take on something new is a life marker
It is a place of beginning
A time of excitement and new energy
Barriers disappear or appear surmountable
Enthusiasm reigns
We know there will be peaks and valleys,
but we are ready for them
Nothing holds us back

When there is dread in your heart or a
weight on your soul, it must be examined
Is the timing right?
Are you sure of your support?
Do you need additional assistance?
Is it all overwhelming?
Are you willing to let go?
To trust the Universe? To surrender?

Remember that you do not give yourself up
You give up to yourself
Not always easy to do,
but definitely worth the effort
The deeper the barrier,
the harder it is to overcome,
but the more gratifying the reward
There are no laurels to rest upon in this work
Each change involves transition

As you move from one place to another,
there will be periods of uncertainty
Allow for them
They are part of the process
They give the process validity

We will cover you with our wings
while you rest
And surround you with love when you wake
Trust not your soul to anyone but you
For the worth of your soul
cannot be measured
We speak for ourselves so that others
may hear the words and build upon them

When the Dalai Lama speaks, people listen
His every word has meaning
His thought process is deep
Developed as it was over many years
Some question his wisdom
Others fear it

The road to such clarity is a long one
The path strewn with obstacles
Only the most tenacious make the journey
Sands shift under your feet
The righteous call you down
Wherever you go,
the winds of change will follow
The quest for knowledge
will beat a path to your door

Retaining dignity, maintaining
balance will be a struggle
Throw not these cautions to the wind
as they are meant as a guide
Neither become discouraged by their words
For if you make this path your own,
there will be beacons along the way
You will not be alone

Fall back a little and regroup
The light shines upon you
as it does upon everyone

Allow it to penetrate your being
and fill up your soul
Ignite your spirit with its energy
Welcome it into your heart
Communicate with it

Rational decision making
and dream making become one
The way of the world
and the Way become one
The 13 tribes were right
None leads us better than we lead
Ourselves but we must work together

So, too, must you find others
to converse with, that you will not be alone
Measure progress in centimeters
as it may come slowly

Start with you
Resonate within
Reconnect
One person, grounded within,
balanced without
Focused on the path ahead
Aware of what has already transpired
and centered in the present
Willing to make the sacrifices
necessary to experience growth

In some respects, an isolated personage
In others an energy center
that emits light and hope

Attracting those at the same level
Passing on comfort and
Encouragement to those in need
Raising awareness
Introducing people to themselves
Sharing words, creating rhythms
Using energy, urging insight into oneself

The role of the teacher
is to offer opportunities
Then step back and watch the student grow
What you present is a menu
from which others may choose
Sometimes adding their own entrees
They will become thoroughly involved

You must remain impartial
On the sidelines ready to assist,
but not part of the process
Being open and nonjudgmental
creates a comfortable space

The Search

Amazing feats can be accomplished
The world can pass beneath you
Problems can be solved
You will never be alone

In the specter of time
lies the answer to all
No longer bound by earthly things
Spirits are free to roam
The lessons learned set forth a plan

Connect yourself with others
in a similar place
Allow yourself to sit at their table
Rest the parts of you that have been stressed
Walk with peaceful spirits and relax

Remember that the object is not
accumulation nor is it being on TV
Acclaim can be a blessing and a curse
Foster those things within you
that can help the world
Reach out to others in His name

Raise no expectations
Promise no results
Keep your focus narrow in the beginning,
for expertise takes time

Worry not about connecting
with the other side
They applaud your every move
For the line is thin

This is enough for today
Wrap yourself up in the future
Let your course unfold
It has begun

$\mathcal{M}$ajor lines of communication
can be opened, if you are willing to hear
The past opens itself up to those who listen
Stories told of long ago
Personages brought to life
are brought to life for a reason
For during life, not all can be told

The world neither understands nor wants to hear
what is in the deep recesses of a heart or mind
Freedom to reveal all comes only when
we are no longer on the Earth plane

The anger, the fears, the joys
The pain that has never been shared
The thoughts that whirl through our heads
The reasons why decisions were made
All are there to be tapped

The process can be long
The road can be a little rough
A lifetime of stories cannot
be written in a day
Write not for the glory it will bring,
but for the story it will tell

Do your homework
Be prepared to become part
of someone else's journey

It is a commitment of your life
The revelations may pierce your soul
The intimacies may break your heart

Once on paper, you will let them go
There are many stories waiting to be told
You are limited only by the time available
We will be waiting to hear from you

*K*eep a clear mind
Watch out for potholes
Line up your ducks
Count them carefully

When you are at a crossroad, opportunities appear
Judge each one carefully before you leap
Be as the lizard who uses all its senses to survive
Examine the corners of your mind
to discover what you really want
Break it down into little pieces

The quality of life must be preserved
Every moment is precious, not to be squandered
Look to your soul for peace
Keep your path uncluttered
As opportunities arise, take only those
that best suit your needs

Your whole being will hum
when the choice is right
Feel it within you
Let the flame rise to its own level
Weigh alternatives carefully
The heaviest one loses

Fulfillment of the soul is paramount
Your spirit needs to be free
Consider all things before making a decision

We race through life,
not looking where we are going
Stopping only when necessary
Colliding with ourselves and others
Wondering why the pieces don't fit
Waiting for things to come together

Questions arise about the meaning of life
How can we be fulfilled?
Why are we here?
The answers can only be found in stillness

Grow not dependent on the advice
of others; think for yourself
Walk not in the shadow of others
Make your own path
The quality of life
The ministry of the soul
Both are of utmost importance

Cry out if you are in pain
Rejoice when you feel joy
Wallow not in sorrow once it has passed
Live each day for itself
For in truth, that is all we have

Do not wait for the sun to shine
or the rain to pass
Choose life, choose harmony

Make every effort to adapt
Learn from every situation
Be open to new experiences
The plan will become clear
and you will move on

$\mathcal{M}$any tasks lie before us,
each with its own priorities
What are yours?
The key to efficiency is having a clear head
Be mindful of those around you
But do not absorb their responsibilities

A cross section of life shows
many tasks at many levels
Importance is relative
The process for eliminating
paperwork is simple
Use it or lose it
Stacks of paper decrease efficiency
Wading through mud is harder
than wading through water

The most difficult task is getting organized
Efforts in this direction are not wasted
A list is good only if it is used
A chart is good only if it is followed

Mental cobwebs must be cleared
All aspects of exercise will accomplish this
Ranting and raving exacerbate the problem
Deep thought, meditation
and mindful silence are helpful
Constant stress, inefficiency and
disorganization are signs of overload
Recognize them

Peg Roberts

Vow to take on nothing else
until the situation has been rectified
It is a downward cycle
The only way to win is to start back up
Lighten the load
Think of your replacement
Work out a plan to help that person cope
Then use it yourself

All goals can be attained in time
Great feats can be accomplished
The best strategy is still planning
but with a different focus
Emphasize the now, deemphasize the then

Let little things slip away
Do away with minutia
Lay out the master plan
Set your large goals
Find the resources and delegate

Watch over your flock like a mother hen
Use outside resources whenever possible
Keep focused on the goal of each project
Maintain realistic timelines
Visualize your outcomes
The resources will follow

As you proceed, seek a calmness within
A serenity that will sustain you
In all ways, seek to be centered
For your existence may depend upon it

The wise ones tell us
there is no peace in turmoil
Internal turmoil manifests itself externally
Take in the energy of the Universe
that your turmoil will be dissipated,
and you will feel the joy of contentment

*Th*e way is different for each person
Some climb mountains
Some descend into valleys
Some walk on a plain

In determining which path is right for you
You must trust your senses,
your intuition and your feelings
Listen to yourself,
for your spirit will speak to you
The message may be loud or so soft
that you wonder if you really heard anything

When you are on the right track
A light will shine in your heart
Your step will be lighter
A great burden will lift from your shoulders
You will feel free
There are no rules to follow but one
Be true to yourself above all others

Your path must not compromise your soul,
for that is your essence
It gives your life meaning
A clear path has meaning for both worlds
It satisfies you within and without
It allows creation and expression,
satisfaction and a sense of worth

You walk with vigor and vitality
Eagerly awaiting
the approach of each new day
You may walk among
the well-known or among the poor
You may develop wealth or merely get by

The method of attaining success is not important
It is the quality of life that matters
How satisfied you are at the end of the day
There will be bumps, stress,
impossible situations to address

But through it all, you will know that solutions will come
Through it all, your soul will be singing your song
You will know that what you are doing is right
You will rise above doubts and frustration,
because a part of you will be at peace

When we strip away the trappings
When we peel off the outer layer
All we have is ourselves
People of the Universe are we
Each with a special job to do
and a mission to fulfill
Listen with your heart and your soul
That you may hear your words
above the din of life
Those who have gone before you will help you
Those who are here will support you
You have only to begin

Bury not the dead with the living
Keep yourself available at all times
Bend not to mounting pressure
For as it goes, so do you

Walk not in the shadows
For you need to be in the light
Making progress can mean standing still
For progression can be mind-boggling

In the twilight, a soft light appears,
sending out its shaft for all to see
Expecting nothing in return
It is simply there for all to enjoy
No timelines, no schedules,
no windows of opportunity
As darkness falls, it fades away
Not gone, for it remains there unseen

Why then do we feel the need to be seen,
to be noticed, to have a place in the spotlight?
Is it because there is a certain place
we are seeking but have not found?
Could it be that a part of us feels misplaced?
Are we discontented with where we are?
Perhaps the answers
aren't as hidden as we think
Perhaps they are right in front of us

If we look at where we are
and how we got there
If we think of where we would like to be
If we speak with those who could be helpful,
and we listen clearly to what they have to say
Then our questions may be answered
and our doubts may be put to rest

The path we think we should follow
may not be our path at all
It may be a temporary stopping point
before we venture on
If your path is strewn with rubble,
you may miss the turn
Simply turn around and make the turn again

In the place between two spaces there is time to breathe
No better place than this to get your bearings
The place is in your mind and needs no invitation
One spot in your comfort zone
A place where prayers can be heard
An alternative resting place
for those who are burdened

When you feel a bump in the road, stop to examine it
Place a marker there before you move on
Another road, another time,
another bump, another opportunity
Put in front of us for our perusal
Cast aside when we are not ready
Seized when we are

Perspective

*N*o ordinary people are we
Held together as we are by strong ties
Nurtured in the bosom of Mother Earth
Each seeing life through our own window frame
Classical figures in a non-classical world

Arise from the darkness where you lie
Greet the coming of a new day
Share your gifts, that they may
bring a little light into the world

For a voice not heard does not exist
A picture not captured is gone forever
And a story untold cannot be repeated
Tell your story to all who will listen
and then listen to theirs
For each of us has gifts to share

Disregard appearances
Look beyond riches or lack of them
See not only with your eyes
but with your heart
Hear not only with your ears
but with your soul
And you will discover
that everyone has worth

A secret to share, an insight, a perspective
An idea that could change the world
Love that could lift us
from the depths of despair

Sometimes buried like a treasure
waiting to be discovered
Sometimes right there for all to see
Sometimes cast aside, unvalued
But they are always there, these gifts
They are our contribution to life
And they are badly needed

For in the end, you see,
there are no ordinary people.
Each of us a special creation of the Universe
Molded on the outside by circumstance
We all originate from the same source

As charming as life may be
It still has its ups and downs
The lessons we learn are forever evolving
We start at a certain place
in the circle to look for answers
The paths we take may not seem connected
The questions we ask may seem not to have answers
The answers we hear may seem to have no meaning

In ancient times a man would till his field
Does this mean that all men must till fields?
People wandered the desert with no permanent homes
Should all the world maintain that lifestyle?
As we challenge ourselves with
such questions, let us remember this:

The rules of this world were made by men
Based upon their simple knowledge
The Earth does not have such rules
She asks only to be respected
The seasons are there for all to see,
unchanging, full of life and beauty
Man must work around them

Before a tree can grow
A seed must be planted
These are the laws of nature
They are not up for discussion

Man, however, bends his rules to meet his needs
The need for an orderly society
The need for safety
The need to procreate

Before the hand can open, it must close
Hands joining together reap benefits for all
For in unity there is strength
The rules of man are like a closed hand
waiting for the opportunity to open
Unaltered by thousands of years of separateness
The law of each land being supreme

Reason tells us to adapt, but change is hard
Tradition plays a major role
The whole, however,
is greater than the sum of its parts

It is time to take a fresh look
To peel away the layers of differences
To look at life as it really is
Not disconnected, not all the same
To look to the Earth for guidance about being
whole as a world, as a society, as individuals
To seek our answers on a different plane
To read the words that are put before us
in a different context

For man and nature to become one
Void of rules that don't count
Recognizing that all paths lead in the same direction
And that we are all part of the same circle

The hope of man lies deep within his chest
Waiting for an opportunity to spring forth
The hope of God, having already sprung,
covers the Universe
In searching for answers,
look to God for assurance and support
But look within for the solution

Allow the hope of man to come forth into the light
For, indeed, it is the light that shows us the way
Put everything into perspective
The pain of a short separation from a loved one
is nothing compared to the pain of death

Looking at a mountain from below
is very different than gazing from the summit
Climb the first rise and then the next
Each time you look back,
your starting point will appear different
Eventually, it will dim
and there will be no reason to look back

We learn more from the mountains we climb
than on our journeys across a plain
We appreciate more the answers we find
than the answers we are given
But know one thing, you are never alone
Universal love will surround you, if you let it
And on the other side, you have a cheering squad

All things are possible
You have only to let them happen
Resistance can be your enemy
Sucking around your feet like muck
Pulling you down into a quagmire
Change can be extremely difficult

Hampered by our fears, real or
imagined and by the lead in our feet
But remember there are two sides to change
Just as there are two sides of a mountain

Eventually, you reach the top
and can enjoy the view on the other side
You need only add a "d" to change
to complete the task
You need not find a whole new word
Depend upon your instincts and
the support of God and those who love you
For the space you find yourself in
will not last forever

The promise of life awaits you
As you begin to move, you will
feel your hope spring forth
There is no way to avoid it
Your burden will shift and begin to lift
You will deal with your fears
and your feet will lighten
And in the words of a wise man:
Those who seek answers deserve the rest
that comes to them

When fog rolls in across the plain,
it changes the perception of the landscape
We sometimes lose our bearings
Tossed pebbles cause ripples
upon the surface of a still pond
So too, do the actions of others affect us

Busy days and busy nights reduce our ability to cope
High expectations of others can lead to disappointment
Stress can make the smallest thing appear large

We become vulnerable
Paranoia in its subtlest form slips in
Each event becomes magnified
Words spoken in ordinary conversation
seem to be aimed at us
Actions that do not meet our expectations
cause anger or pain

Remember that no one's world revolves around us
That our stresses and strains belong only to us
If the issue that angered or disappointed
is important, address it
If it is of no consequence, let it go

External reactions reflect internal unease
If you are at the end of your emotional rope,
sort through your feelings
Are you taking care of yourself?
Are your relationships in need of tweaking?

Look at your expectations of others
Are they reasonable or simply a reflection
of what you want to happen?
Does anyone besides you
know that they exist?

If stress has brought you to this point,
examine it carefully
How much is self-imposed?
What is your stress comfort level?
How much is imposed by others?

The action that caused the reaction is not the issue
It is the spark that lit a smoldering ember
The reaction is a signal not to be ignored
For if it is not dealt with,
the fire inside will continue to grow
Each reaction will be more pronounced
The cause will burn deeper
inside you as the flame rises

Heed these signals as you would a traffic light
Slow down to see what is happening in your life
Stop for a while to look inside
Then move ahead when the way is clear

*A*s life progresses,
our heads become cluttered
Seldom do we sort through it all
Perceptions are based on experience
Some are deeply rooted
and are hard to change
Finding their source is
like solving a mystery

A fear may come from a childhood experience
that is not easily remembered
A prejudice may be rooted
in the atmosphere of our surroundings
An attitude can be based on a perception
of how the world treats us
When we are young,
the adults in our lives shape our perceptions
As we grow, we develop our own

Simple at first, like right or wrong,
good and bad, our heads are soon filled
We spend the rest of our lives, consciously or
unconsciously, filtering through them

We have an external perception of how people see us
We have an internal perception of ourselves
In reality, we see ourselves as we <u>think</u> others see us
Our self-esteem limits or expands our internal perception

Sometimes the pictures change
Sometimes they do not; we make the choice
A childhood fear can be overcome
A prejudice, once examined, can dissipate
The lines between wrong and right become blurred

As the seasons change, so do our perceptions
We realize that other people's perceptions of us
are not as important as our own
That our sense of self-worth comes
from the inside not the outside
That we may not be comfortable
with our family's perception of the world
That bad experiences will shatter
our lives, only if we let them
That those who love us want what is best for us,
but may not know what that is
That true friends respect our decisions
That every perspective we have
should be examined once in a while

They are challenged by wisdom and experience
If we are open to change, we will allow old perceptions
to be replaced with new ones
We will recognize that we are held back
by the perceptions we refuse to examine
That our strength comes
from the perceptions we know to be valid
That we are freed from those we let go
Perceptions reside in our heads
It is up to us to clean the residence

Peg Roberts   **90**

The place where you are
is the place where you are
There is nothing you can do
to get away from it
See it through to its conclusion

Coming as we do from a place of peace
It is sometimes difficult to deal with stress
For stress puts demands on our body
and makes us uncomfortable
Anxiety sucks the life from us
and puts us on edge
The solution is not always simple to see
at first, yet it is always there

Walk among the pine trees in the forest
Straight and tall they stand
Sheltering each other from the wind
They appear to have limited experience
for they cannot move
But they are wise, these trees
From their vantage point
they have a broad perspective
Connected as they are
to the earth and the sky
Their roots sink deep to give them stability
Yet their boughs flutter freely in the breeze
high above the forest floor

Their cones drop from great heights undamaged,
with the seeds of the next generation of trees
It is their life cycle

As they grow, they become stronger
When they are young, they bend
and twist in the breeze
Age only improves them

Straight and tall they stand,
reaching up to the heavens
Surviving all types of weather
despite their inability to move
Could we not then learn
from the life cycle of a tree?

When the winds of life fan us and
sometimes blow us around, we can be strong
Strong roots and ties give us a solid
foundation from which to develop
They keep us from drifting away,
yet they allow us to move about freely
Their deepness grounds us,
yet allows our spirits to fly
Our experience leads to wisdom
A wisdom born of pain and fear,
joy and sorrow, laughter and tears

We don't always know what is right
But are pretty sure of what is wrong
We can still be intimidated
We are continually challenged

Each incident bringing with it
its own experience
Some pleasant, some not
Some fruitful, some not
Some successful, some not
But all with a message, a lesson
or an opportunity sent to us
courtesy of the Universe

Listen for the message
as hidden as it may appear to be
Be open to learning life's lessons
when they are given to you
Seize the opportunities
that appear seemingly from nowhere
For messages heard will give you insight
Lessons learned will lead you in the right direction
and opportunities taken will lead to fulfillment

*T*he small blessings in life often go unnoticed
We eagerly await our children's first steps
But take for granted that they will always walk
We do not realize the places their feet will take them
They will patter down the hall and into our hearts
Run across a playground and into our arms
Skip down the street holding our hands
Climb aboard the school bus
waving good-bye

Later, they tiptoe into our rooms
to bring us a surprise
Crawl into our laps seeking consolation
Our babes, our pride and joy, now half grown,
then race on to new adventures
Jump through their own hoops
Stumble, fall and falter as their steps
take them on their own journeys

Sometimes we want to save them
but have to let them fall
Just when we want to hold on tight,
we have to let them go
Suddenly, it seems,
young men and women appear
Marching to their own drummers
Setting their own courses
Tossing graduation caps into the air

Walking down the aisle
Holding the hand of another
Eagerly awaiting their child's first step
Beginning the journey of their lives
We watch with such pride
They have made themselves
They are nearly complete
And it all started with one small step

Sadness, in all its forms,
springs from many sources
Fear not the path you tread
or the obstacles that are in the way
They are but small inconveniences

No parent can hear the anger
of their child and be unaffected
It is like laying a rod across a bare back
The sting of the words and sadness at their source
combine into a special melancholy
But wallowing in that pain is not an option
Let it blow past you
Stand aside to avoid the blow

Their feelings are valid, but they are theirs
Their hurt is genuine, but what of yours?
Did you not give up everything for them?
Did you not dedicate your life
to taking care of them?
What of your hurt? Your anger?
Must it always come second
to the needs of your children?

In the heat of battle, both sides charge
Progress takes place at the negotiating table
So, too, with families
Venting is important

Precious are the times
you get to spend together
Guard them carefully, for the time will come
when the bird will fly from the nest
Growing up is a continuing process
One never quite makes it

As we go forth into the world
it's nice to know that the nest is still there
Sometimes there is
a pressing need to stand alone
Loss is a matter of degree
If you choose to be on your own,
you are no longer considered to be a child
If you choose to maintain your status as a child,
you forfeit the opportunity for independence

A parent's role is never easy
We are always on the cusp
Trying to do the right thing but never sure
We pray for our children when they are sick
and for ourselves when they are well
They are our greatest joy, but their
slightest rejection can tear us apart

When they are small,
we spin a tight web to keep them safe
As they grow, it is their job to tear it asunder
We make them the center of our world;

Yet criticize that they are self-centered
It's a rocky road we travel
but one that has many possibilities

We must be strong as steel but bend as a willow
We must protect but not smother
Most of all, we must know
when to hold on and when to let go
We have been entrusted with a precious life
It is our job to encourage growth and
help these children realize their dreams

In the process, we surrender our freedom
and experience a love like no other
We are wrapped around their fingers
from the moment they are born
Their love can make us feel whole
As they fly from the nest, our hearts
are breaking and overflowing at the same time
We are bursting with pride and feeling a certain sorrow

Of none of this are they aware
And that's as it should be
We depend upon the pattern of the ages
That once well established in their own lives
They will have time to spend with us
A pattern that is part of the ebb and flow of life

Age brings understanding, as we now realize
Youth, with the world at its feet, waits for no one
Elders watch, sometimes marveling
Often encouraging

Sometimes reminiscing
Ready to share a bit of wisdom
when the time is right

Life truly is a circle
It cannot be a straight line
We live, we laugh, we cry, we love
We share each other's passions and sorrows
We are a family

*I*n 20 years, your children will be different people
The value of their pain must be recognized
Give them the patience they deserve
A wide berth is best

As they progress, they will
shed their protective skin like the layers of an onion
Self-maintenance is of grave importance right now
Support from a distance may be most effective
They are, after all, grown adults

Keep your arm around them,
but do not squeeze tightly
The healing can take place
regardless of your touch

Visit with their souls and speak on a different level
If the spirit is not receptive, take it no further
for intrusion is not the goal

Even as you speak, be mindful the response
Sometimes the ones we love the most
have the hardest time accepting
Each will come in their own time
The ball has been tossed
Eventually it will be caught

Worry and stress on your part
will only add to the tension
Let it go

Let frustration fade
Be aware but let worry drain from the picture
Your prayers are always heard
"Doing your own thing" can have good results

The passage of time brings many changes
What once was, no longer is
What has never been, will now be
What has passed seems better
or worse than it really was
What is, is often overlooked
as we look ahead or back

We lead our children
from the day they are born
Protecting and teaching them
Showing them the way
They are our life's blood
Encouraged by us, cheered on
We see their lives unfold
Soon they are gone
Off on their own adventures
Unaware of the impact
this change has on our lives

We move on to our own adventures
But part of us hangs back
Hoping, wanting, needing to be needed
Knowing that we must move on
But feeling like part of us is missing
In our heads, we feel that it is silly
But our hearts know otherwise

New joys enter our lives
Brought to us by the new generation
Our new roles are less demanding
Our experience is sometimes valued, sometimes not
We develop new life interests
Our heads still understand the change
better than our hearts, but we move on

Decisions

The twain shall finally meet for you
The tide will rise
Forecasts for a bright spring are clear
When nature calls, obey

The right path may not seem right
For its course may steer you in a new direction
Praise those who have followed you well,
before you move on

In your darkness, a light shall appear
It is the light of your future
Sometimes bright, sometimes dim
It is there for you
Making decisions can be the hardest part

As we go through life,
we tend to maintain the status quo
Separating from the crowd can be difficult
The question of devotion is at hand
Must you forever remain connected to the past?
Or is it time to shed the shackles and move on?

The answer lies within you
It cannot be voiced by another
The rod and the staff may comfort you
The words of change may swirl around you
But the decisions are yours to make

Harmony and peace in your world
matter not, if they come not from within
Waiting for a bus that does not
travel on your street is fruitless

Taking a train just because it's there
may not get you to your destination
When you know where you want to go,
the path will be clear
You will be one with your decision

Raging rivers will not stop you
Nor will petty complaints get in your way
For from within will ring the knowledge
that you are right
You will have chosen well
A new adventure awaits you
Begin as soon as you are ready

Decisions, once made, can always be changed
The lesser of two evils is not a good basis
on which to decide
Crawling along a ridge pales
next to jumping off a cliff

Reason and emotion often conflict
Like magnetic energy, they repel each other
Each representing a different point of view
One looking at situations as they are
The other seeing how it could be
under different circumstances

Consider the ancient nomad whose water hole dried up
To live, he had to move on, but part of him wanted to stay
To go meant leaving behind a way of life
that centered around the water hole
Staying meant trying to maintain
a lifestyle without the mainstay
Like baking a cake with no flour

The process of change is not without pain
It is not unlike birth - going from a warm comfortable
space through a dark tunnel and out into the light
We are forced to change our focus
Sometimes our focus is changed for us
We get stuck because moving on means
leaving what is dear along with what is not
The trick is to see where we are going
when change is inevitable

Before making a decision,
find a good reason for making it
Will it benefit anyone?
Will it hurt anyone?
How will it affect you?

There must be a point to doing something
What are your objectives?
Will your decision
affect your internal balance?
Of all the questions,
this may be the most important

For in sharing what you do,
you may change your way of life
You must decide if the possible gains
outweigh possible losses
In a hundred years, the world will be different,
but the words will be the same
Once written, they will not change
The benefit to man will always be there

In developing your art, you must stay focused,
lest you turn away from the gift
In going to the next level,
there are sacrifices to be made
Time and energy to be spent
A wise crone limits her exposure,
because she knows her limits

Starting small may be best
for it is controllable
Remember not to jeopardize
yourself for the gain
Involve only people who care about you
Let them handle the affairs, for that is not your job

Ease into the market, lest you be overcome
The time is right whenever you are
Share your talent, but do not sell your soul
It is your core and is not for sale
If others find their own,
they will have no need for yours
A positive outcome is in the offing,
if you stay on track

The passage of time will not lessen the impact
The appropriate time to address an issue may never come
Steppingstones will be placed before you
Use them to find your way
In all cases, be gentle

Stay in touch with your own soul
Be open and honest
Let others know your feelings
For this has been a painful process
Tears upon your cheeks
may say more than a thousand words
Don't be afraid to let them fall

The reactions may be varied
Give others space; walk beside them in silence
Comfort them if they reach out; let any anger blow by you
Be clear about your decision
The shock may not be as great as you think

As time goes by, the adjustment will take place
Remember, the process has been difficult and long
The decision not made lightly or without pain
They need to hear that

There were good times
Moving on is not an indication of failure
They need to hear that, too
Use your natural instincts
They always work well and will help
you through a difficult time

In the twinkling of an eye, our past appears
Bringing with it all its baggage
The plan is never crystal clear
The way is clear but never the plan
Your spirit wants one thing;
your mind another

Bridging the gap is a challenge
Keeping your feet on the ground is important,
as is feeding your soul
Weigh the alternatives carefully
but with a twist
Is crossing the road
just to get to the other side worthwhile?
Claim victory for yourself wherever it lies
When an opportunity appears, let it ride
Create within yourself a space
where you can go to mull it over

Be at peace with yourself
Let not a challenge scare you
Look at it squarely in its own right
Know within yourself where you are going
Face your own demons
Decide what you need
and what is best for you

When the fit is right, you will know
At that point, listen to your gut
Be not led by those who wish to lead you
Move silently through your own process
Find your center and do not lose track of it
The way is always clear
It is up to you to find it

$\mathcal{A}$t each point in the road of life,
we are faced with choices
Making the "right" choice is not easy
and sometimes not necessary
Sometimes there is no right or wrong
Is it wrong to choose happiness over sadness?
Is it right to choose work over play?
We make these choices every day

We choose to be open or closed
when we interact with each other
The choices we make affect others
If we are open, they will feel welcome
If we are distant, they may feel alienated
This sets up choices for them

To move, to change jobs,
to enter into a relationship
Each choice takes us down a different path
What appears in retrospect to be a poor choice
may have provided a valuable lesson
Each of us, in our own way,
follows our own path
For some, the twists and turns are many
For others, they are few

When seeking counsel,
remember to touch base with yourself
For we are all wise in our own ways

Listen to your heart as the song it sings
may include a clue
Consider your peace of mind
and how it will be affected
Pray to your God
as you will never be let down
Challenge your mind to connect
with your soul
For that bond may be
the most powerful of all
Choices are not irrevocable,
but they are unending
Hone your skills, as they are much needed

*T*he quality of life stems not
from what we have
But from what we do with what we have
If sharing is important to you,
then you should share
Words upon a paper mean nothing
if no one reads them
Pictures on a wall mean nothing
if no one sees them
If a man grows crops, but does not
get them to market, they are lost

Remember this: the choice is always yours
You may act or take no action
If acting brings you pleasure, then proceed
If the greatest satisfaction comes from
keeping to yourself, then take no action
For what you do in life
is an outgrowth of your spirit
It must feel right inside

For it does no good to act,
if that action is uncomfortable
Whatever you do, keep a clear head and a clear mind
Stay connected to yourself and the Universe
Choose from untold possibilities
The sky is the limit,
but you must remain centered

There is stress in all situations,
no matter how positive
Inner peace and strength make it manageable
If the time has come to move ahead,
choose your path carefully
Gather around you those who truly care,
for the ride may be bumpy
Clasp your hands to your breast,
take a deep breath and proceed

$\mathcal{A}$ ray of light will shine upon you and guide you
There are no easy answers, as you well know
As you contemplate change,
ask yourself what you <u>need</u> to exist,
what compromises you are willing to make
Talk with yourself about your heart's desire
Is there a way to incorporate it?
Must you always be responsible for everything?

Make yourself available to new thoughts and ideas
Take advantage of the connections you have
Keep the lines of communication open to others,
but more especially with yourself
For you are the one who has to make the decision
Make sure it feels right inside

Sacrifice not the essence of your soul for the position
Jump not at the first offer for the sake of change
Listen not to the buzz of the world,
but to your heart and soul
How does your stomach feel?
What lessens the weight on your shoulders?
Is there excitement in the air?

Start making the transition now
before a decision is made
Examine who you are
Take steps to lessen your load
and decrease your presence

Increase productivity in other areas
Take a chance on something new
Go down an old familiar road
Reconnect with old friends
Make new ones
Do whatever feels right

There will be stresses
Nothing worthwhile comes without stress,
but healthy stresses are productive
They motivate; they do not weigh you down
Set your goal, lay out a timetable, develop your plan
Be realistic, but lofty;
Reach for the stars,
but be ready to settle for the moon
Listen to yourself
Listen to yourself
Listen to yourself
For within you are the answers
Trust yourself with the decision
For in the end, you are all you have

*T*he sweetness of life is to be savored
Like fine wine, it rolls across your tongue
Like the fragrance of a rose on a summer day

The crush of everyday life sometimes blots it out
Leaving us with a sour taste in our mouths
Wondering if that's all there is

Stop what you are doing when that happens
Look around you and observe your physical space
Is it comfortable?
Listen to your breathing. Is it regular?
Does the air feel heavy or light?
Check in with your body
Is the tension coming from
within or without?

Think about someone you love
What would you say to them
if they were in this situation?
Take your own advice
Create for yourself a space that is yours
Open the windows to clear the air

As you continue your journey, remember:
Your journey is your own
You get to choose the course
but not always the circumstances
Internal strife manifests itself externally

Peace and tranquility reflect
back upon you also
Attitude is a matter of choice
and choices have consequences
Lessons once learned need not be repeated
Make your choices wisely
Make them your own
That you may savor the sweetness of life

Remind yourself of how
and why a decision was made
Carry those thoughts with you
Light a candle for hope
Set the table for company

Move forward with your plan
Taking the first step is always the hardest
Pounce like a kitten on a ball
The reasons may not be clear
but will make sense eventually

Proceed with a light heart
For the fog will be lifting soon
As always, use your best judgment
in making decisions
Consult with others,
but decide for yourself

Paths are not walkways
as much as they are guideposts
Beacons that show the way
Opportunities for the taking
Crossroads where decisions are made
Each decision accompanied by its own beacons,
opportunities and more crossroads

Our choices define our lives
Our lives are a reflection of the journey we take
The stress of bad times actually strengthens us
The lessons we learn straighten our backs

In the jungle, there are dangers everywhere,
yet tribes live safely
In the heat of the desert, families thrive
On steep mountain slopes, life abounds
We are all in our places
We survive, because we adapt to our surroundings
We flourish when our hearts are full
and wither when they are not

The moment we let go, our hearts begin their song
Small at first, it becomes increasingly louder,
accompanied by joy
The joy of laughter, the joy of freedom
the joy of independence, the joy of self-reliance
All registering at different times and different levels
All supporting us as we move ahead
Creating a backdrop against which we create life
Giving us comfort when our way is not clear
Moving us forward when we would rather stand still
Providing solace when there are tears

An angel of mercy
that stays with us through thick and thin
A support system that cannot fail
The many faces of ourselves, often hidden from view,
now released from bondage and allowed to expand
Our futures are our own

Emotions

Making a day glow is a work of art
that comes from inside
For all days are the same, each with 24 hours
It is the perception that is different
We welcome some days and dread others
depending on their content
Why not appreciate the day for itself?
The time, once gone, can never be recovered
Our lives are wrapped in it

Consider the candy wrapper
Quickly discarded for the contents inside
Yet without it, what would the candy be like?
Clothing creates an image on the outside,
but has nothing to do with the inside of a person
Yet it keeps us warm and dry

Each part of our lives has a place
Some are more welcome than others
We are quick to discard or push aside
those parts that are harder to deal with

A garden, once planted, is beautiful
But it is the hard work and labor
that made beauty possible
Physical problems, while sometimes
unpleasant, are concrete
The emotions are a different story

Our experiences dictate our reactions
Our emotions are wrapped inside them
In our search for answers, we are quick to
discard these wrappers to examine the emotions

In what is your anger wrapped?
A sense of injustice?
What cloaks your sadness?
Was it stifled in the past or discounted?
What does happiness mean to you?
Is it a natural occurrence
or a harbinger of bad times ahead?

The lesson to be learned is this:
Each of us has our own set of experiences
that influence our lives
Just like candy wrappers, they protect us
They give validity to our reactions
but they can also get in our way of living

We must appreciate them for what they are
Be thankful for the jobs they have done
Validate their importance
Keep them in case we need them
for future reference
But get on with the business
of eating the candy bar
For joy, sadness, anger, compassion
and happiness are the ingredients of life

*T*ears are but symbols of our grief
They spill from our eyes with great abandon
Like a spring shower
A soft weeping for those who have passed
For things as they are
For life as it could be
Or like a summer storm, hot and burning
Filled with anger and frustration

Sometimes shed with others
Often shed alone
In the pit of our grief
They are our only outlet

Oh, tears, bring us the relief we seek
Help us loosen the shackles of the past
and move us into the future
Let your salty brine help us to move on

The source of our anger,
the well from which it rises,
is often stoked by current affairs
In stressful times,
one is more easily provoked
A fire in your belly, a body flush
caused by a sense of injustice
A sharp tongue lashing out at those
who make you feel bad
Sometimes justified; sometimes not

Anger is like a grain of sand
within an oyster shell
An irritant that we want to get rid of
Just as the oyster coats the grain of sand
We sometimes protect ourselves from anger
We build walls, force ourselves to forget
No matter how beautiful the pearl,
the grain of sand is still inside

When anger seemingly comes from nowhere
When you are easily offended by what others say
Begin to look for the grain of sand
For it may be the source of your discomfort
Have you let others make decisions
for you without speaking up?
Have you swallowed your feelings,
because you didn't want to make waves?

Were situations forced upon you
over which you had no control?

Think about it; trace it back
Anger is a natural human emotion
You are human

The soul does not need anger
When others make you angry, look inside
When you become annoyed, look inside
Take a deep breath and let it out slowly

Remove yourself from the situation
and think about the grain of sand
Was it deposited earlier in the day
when you weren't watching?
Or is this situation
one that reoccurs regularly?
Finding the irritant and
flushing it away will free you
Once let go, a burden can
no longer weigh you down
Once broken, an old pattern
will not be repeated

Success may be instantaneous,
or it may take a while
Life's lessons are not always easy to learn
But once learned, they will not be forgotten
The real pearl is the wisdom
we gain that has love at its center

Sometimes I look to the Heavens
and wonder where you are
You struggled so before you left
A mother wanting the best for her children
A sister, a daughter, an almost great aunt
connected to the unborn babe

The frustration and pain
You dealt with it all
In the end, peace descended upon you
You slipped away gently to those who were waiting
No longer here in body, you remain in our hearts

In the morning mist that hangs over a pond,
I see your love for beauty
The Great Plains of South Dakota shall forever
embody your search for truth
When I go to the beach, I take you with me
For that is truly your home
As times passes, you stay forever young
An inspiration to many, loved by all

At times you walk beside me,
for I can feel your presence
You are dear
You are sweet
You are missed

A bright light gone from this life,
but shining forth in another dimension
Waiting for us all on the other side

Peg Roberts   **132**

*L*ove knows no boundaries
For the well from which it springs is eternal
We love a sunny day
We love a starry sky
We love life

The look of a child is pure, untainted by
the vagaries of life, with no conditions
Little arms encircling your neck
A soft warm cheek pressed next to yours
How good that makes us feel!

The bond between friends, sometimes strained
by time and distance, remains strong
Fed by secrets, loyalty and commitment
A special love indeed

The touch of a lover makes you come alive
and soar to the heavens
You stare into each other's eyes
and communicate without saying a word
So connected that you nearly become one
Such love is worth any sacrifice, for it is rare

Perhaps the most perfect love is that of a parent
Always needed, often rejected
It remains constant through good times and bad
A parent's love is all encompassing
There to make a scraped knee better or mend a broken heart
A commitment for life

Your child is someone special, always your child
No matter how old, no matter how far away

Sisters and brothers are unique
Sometimes in competition
Sometimes at each other's throats
They have a very special bond
Confidants, conspirators, defenders of each other
They will stand together against the world
despite their differences

The types of love are many
All are precious and must be nurtured
Take them not for granted
lest they slip through your fingers
Walls built to keep out the world
can also keep out those we love

Remember the unconditional love of a child
Value the strength that comes from the love of a friend
Allow yourself the intimacy of having a lover
Give your mother a call
She will always be there for you
Reminisce about your childhood
with your brothers and sisters
The experience will draw you together

It is never too late
There are no deadlines
The only restrictions are those imposed by you
Open your heart to those you love
That you may be fulfilled

Peg Roberts   **134**

Once a crisis has passed
Walk in your own shoes
You cannot take care of the world
As the tide rises,
so does the chance of flooding

As you sift through your guilt
As you look at relationships
Be aware
Let the chaff blow away
Look at the core
Keeping promises does not
mean giving up your life

It is all a matter of degree
The degree to which you are willing to bend
The degree to which paths cross
The degree to which others
invite you into their lives
The degree to which you are
the right person at the time

Guilt alone is not a reason to respond
Waiting in the wings as a backup can be effective,
if they know you are there
Whatever you can do has to be enough
The time will come
when the effort will flow freely
The stress of other situations will diminish

In the meantime,
Drop a note, send a card, write a letter
Just keep in touch

Action by requirement won't work
The way will be clear when the time is right
Pace yourself, for your plate is heavy
and the air is heavy with unresolved differences

Once things are settled,
Once the air is cleared
Opportunities will arise
Let others take the lead for now
Your time will come

*T*he road to happiness has many twists and turns
The promise of the future lies within you
You have come together as a couple
and will soon become husband and wife

May the sun shine on you both as you
embark on this wonderful journey
May you find the strength to lean
on each other in times of sorrow
The wisdom to recognize
the special gifts you share
And a profound joy in
being together day after day

Nurture your love
with patience and understanding
For happiness is not at the end of the road
It is waiting at every twist and turn
Take advantage of every opportunity
to share it

Let the spirit of your souls
come forth and lead the way
You are both dear children now to many
We all want only the best for you
Your lives are your own
and that is how it should be
Just remember that we are always
here in the wings if you need us

Inner Growth

*Y*et there is darkness to occur
before the dawn appears
Ever the tides increase
Rising higher every day
Storm clouds gathering over distant
shores continue to be a threat
Dressing up ugly packages
does not change the contents

Be sensitive to those around you
Pull them to your breast
that they may revel in your love
Work together to solve problems
Find a way to make paths meet
Look into the eyes and hearts of friends
Take the time needed to share a moment

Wander not away from your humanness,
for it serves you well
It is a platform from which to speak
A holy place, within which you are sheltered
The doing is important
Proceed at once, but do not hurry

Opening yourself to Spirit is the way,
Of all things accomplished,
this will be most important
Waste not what time you have
Nor let the stove grow cold

Yours is a most important task
One that is well needed and sought
As time permits, prepare

Stay not in the place of indecision,
for it limits you
Wait not for doors to open,
for you must knock first

In relationships, be fair
Wrench not your soul from its roots
to please another
Neither let your soul be wrenched
True friendship outlasts all else
Be open to it; hear its call

Do not wash your hands of the world
as you know it
Only those parts that do not fit
As things settle, the taste will be sweet
You will feel comfort in your home,
satisfaction in your work
and a lightness in your heart

*A*s night descends
upon the rolling plain,
a bird appears
Its feathers silhouetted
against the almost dark sky
Searching for a place to rest,
it settles upon a solitary tree
From where did it come?
Where is it headed?
The answers matter not,
as all that is important is where it is

In the early glow of dawn, the bird awakens,
surveys its surroundings and flies away,
happy for the brief respite and ready for the new day
Neither the rolling plain nor the tree had changed
But both were different from having been graced by the
presence of the bird

Wherever we go
Whatever we do
We make a difference
Our presence makes an impact
Our words fill the air
We change nothing, but things
are different for us having been there

The roads we travel have many twists and turns
They take us places that we never dreamed of
They offer us limitless opportunities
This trip is our life

Some say it was planned by us
Some that it was planned for us
Some that there is no plan
The question is: Are we making
the most of it?
Are we focused in the right direction for us?
Are we in touch with our Selves?
Do we connect with our Souls?
The way to your heart is through your soul

Write yourself a love letter
That you may see the beauty of your Spirit
Let go of the burdens weighing you down
that you may be free
Breathe deeply that you may
feel the energy of the Universe

Ground yourself in the present
but reach out to the future
As you continue your journey
Remember that you are special
and that you are never alone

_L_ook into the corners of your heart
→ Dust off the oldest book in your library ←
Create a vision of how you would
like things to be
Collect your thoughts

The twists and turns of the paths we follow
are what make life interesting
Cast aside the pettiness of playmates
Leap across boundaries
to maintain your faith in man
Register your complaints with the one
who has the answers
Rest your head upon the pillow of peace
that your inner soul may be recharged
Linger in a quiet place by a quiet pool
to calm yourself

Connect with your center
Ask yourself questions and then listen
The answers will come from within
For your soul is the channel of the Universe.
It is your connection to beyond
It will never fail you, if you but listen
The answers to your questions in your heart
are to be found in the depths of your soul

The trail before us is long and winding
It leads and we follow
In the silence of a quiet afternoon,
you will sing your song
In the stillness of a summer evening,
you will receive your message

The likelihood of fame is remote,
but the power of ignominy is great
One by one they will come to you,
seeking information and reassurance
Serve them well

Their needs are those of troubled souls
The innermost part of you will respond
Put aside your fears and open your soul
The darkness cannot descend upon you

In all things, there can be danger
Depend not upon the advice of others
Listen instead, to what comes from inside
Stay close to those you love
and those who love you

The course of life may change,
but your gifts will go with you
Resonance with the Universe is everything
A little girl who loves her mother
is a sacred child, to be emulated

Connect with your little girl
and your mother, the Great Mother
For the openness of a child and
the wisdom of mother make all things possible

You need not extend yourself, only reach within
The mythic crone lives on through those who believe
Crone wisdom is passed on silently
from one generation to the next
through those who are open
Be such a vessel
The wisdom awaits

A little hand is gently tugging on your shirt
Your Mother is pulling you to her breast
The gentleness is waiting to descend upon you
Waste not your time upon the mundane
Walk not among the frivolous,
for your work awaits you

The curtain is rising on the rest of your life.
You are the author of your script
Solitude and stillness will be your friends
Your circle of friends will grow, yet remain intimate
Those few who really know you will revere your ways

The sacred will become real
and the real will become sacred
As with all things, it will be a process
The light shines brightly within you
Create the surroundings that you need
Bless the earth and the stars
Settle in and let yourself unfold

As you enter the sanctuary,
a man will appear beside you
His presence guarantees your safety
For the ways of the world can be wicked
Into each life must flow problems
They provide opportunities for growth
Sometimes the opportunity is so great
that we cannot handle it

We separate from our loved ones, our world,
but most importantly, from ourselves
There are no limits to what we can handle
if we are connected to ourselves
We are connected at birth
and through childhood
Worldliness pulls us away
Our humanness leads us in other directions

As we seek to protect ourselves from human pain,
we sometimes lose the connection
Guard this spiritual umbilical cord
Be open to receiving its nourishment
For through it comes the source of all love
The seeds of forgiveness
The light in your soul
and your connection to the Universe

Peg Roberts   **148**

It is the pot of gold at the end of the rainbow
Your own private support system
Available to each of us,
regardless of wealth or position
Wanting nothing from us in return,
It guarantees our spiritual well-being
and provides a haven from the world
A sanctuary for the soul

*B*y bread alone, man does not live
For it is the many who make life possible
Those who are seen and those unseen
When the time is right you, too, will know

Just as majestic mountains
take away your breath so do the faces of God
In all things, be patient, for through
your patience you will begin to see
These words are sent with love and compassion
Do not get bogged down with their meaning
Continue along your path
Wear your heart upon your sleeve
That all may see from where you are coming

From this point hence, you shall know my name
It will come to you on the wind as a riding horse
Sent by your ancestors to show the way
Thought connected to thought, action to action
All intertwined in a connection to be savored
Strength from your source, wisdom for your center
I am the Rising Star

Calling up spirits is delicate work, not for everyone
Connecting with another realm is a different matter
The Ancient Ones do speak to some to share their wisdom
The calm and the wisdom you seek is already there

There are those who visit you now
but make not their presence known
Honor their presence
In times of stress, lean on them
It is not a sign of weakness
They will hold you in their arms
and let you sleep
Comfort you when you are in pain
Ease your sorrow

In the beginning, there were no barriers
between those here and those there
Crossing over was common
The art was not maintained
The capability lost to all but a few
For those who have it, it is a gift to be discovered

Come to the center of the Universe
Toss aside fear and apprehension
Let old barriers fall away
Let your soul be the master, your guide
Connect with yourself first; the rest will follow
The day awaits you; grace it with your presence

*A*t the edge of the wood,
in the first mist of dawn, stands a legend
It is a story as old as time
A story of power and love, of blossoming friendship,
the likes of which no man now knows
The lamb, the sheep and the wolf all laid together
Creatures big and small lived together

From somewhere on high came
the knowledge that all would be well
Self-knowledge was given to those who listened
that they would use it wisely
Assuaging problems and giving hope

In these times, remember the legend,
for it is not so far away
Giving of yourself is never wrong
Believing in yourself is always right
The heights to which you can rise are not limited

Reach out to the stars
that they may envelop you
Bring home their energy
Absorb the peace
Move forward carrying it with you
to another level
Resonate
Release the power within you

Love all who come to you, for they will come
Loosen the shackles that bind you
that you will be free
Let the power go before you
Let the light guide you
Let the spirit be your own

Wind up your life as it is passing quickly
There will never be enough time
to do all that you want to do
The presence of angels shall steer your path
Let them show you the way
Walk with them
Talk with them
Hear what they have to say

There is much for you to do,
if you are willing
Look to the east for guidance and the west
for resolve that you may forge ahead
As you climb your mountains,
take time to enjoy each plateau
for the journey is meant to have meaning

Relish each encounter
that you may learn as much as you teach
Curb your appetite for things that are not beneficial
That you may savor the delicacy of those things that are

Listen, listen, listen for the messages that are always there
There is wisdom all around you
Walk not in circles, once the path is clear
There is no place for hesitation
We are behind you, above you and below you
We welcome our connection with you
as you continue your journey

The ways in which our minds work can be mysterious
We weave our own webs as we wend our way through life
The bottom of the barrel, the top of the heap
We've all been in both places
Both affect our lives

The constant din of the human
world can wreak havoc
It drowns out the silence
We become attuned to it instead of ourselves
We climb ladders of success
Focus on material goods
Sacrifice some of our deepest wishes
Block out some of our dreams
Tell ourselves that what we are doing
is most necessary

Our real work is to use the world to develop our souls
Basing all we do on what comes from within
Being guided by those who are there to help
We are connected to it
when we are young, when we are new
Life's circumstances can change all that
We become connected to our physical world
and lose pieces of our Selves
A process that is gradual and varies in degree

We never totally lose the connection
for there's no way to completely sever the tie
Some maintain it quite well; others slip further away
The struggle to return home underlies life's turmoil
Each external need reflecting the need
to connect with ourselves
For if we do not love ourselves,
no human love can ever fill the void
If we do not value our spiritual worth, no amount
of earthly success will make us feel complete

Only when we connect with our deepest
inner being, can we shut out the earthly din
Only when a balance is struck between
our humanness and our souls, will we be at peace
For only then will we be free to pick and choose
the parts of our lives that will support our internal journey
To realize that they are there to be
used by us and not to rule us
That every part of the human earth experience
is beneficial, if put in the right context
That none of it is so important
that it can't be let go

We learn great lessons from life, if we are open to them
Lessons that complement our soul's development
Release yourself, not from your earthly ties
but from the earthly ties that bind you
For your spirit needs to fly
You can have your cake and eat it, too
Just remember that the sweetness in life
is directly connected to the sweetness in your soul

Peg Roberts   156

*P*repare yourself for the coming onslaught
The stakes are high
The way of the world is not always
the way of the Universe
Proceed with caution, but with an open mind
Souls are gentle, but have great power
Soul power is universal
Its source is from the Oneness

Vast is the knowledge to be passed on
Few are there who are ready to receive it
The range of experiences is great
What is true for one may not be true for another
Personal connection, once established, is always there
Seeing spirits, hearing voices, crossing from
one side to the other are possible

The core is the connection
There are no restrictions
Visitors come and go at will
Even as we speak, they watch over us
Some having recently crossed
Some who have not
All are available when needed
The creation of new knowledge
is not necessary, as all knowledge is there
The vastness of which cannot be comprehended
The connection is the key

Even those who do not believe are often connected
The progress of man races on
Aided on the one hand by those who have tapped in
Hindered on the other by those who have not
Those who are here to help need only to be asked
Their gentle guidance can often be felt
They are a vast resource

Master the mundane
before proceeding to the exotic
Each person is in their own place
The energy, although there for everyone,
can be perceived differently
There is so much to learn,
so much to experience

Let not the paths of others alter yours,
as it is not productive
Take from others what can be used
and let the rest go
If all the world loved blue, red would be missed
Just as it takes all the colors to make a painting
It takes all the experiences to appreciate the Universe

The restlessness you feel, and your lack of motivation
are the price you pay for being disconnected
The more you drift away from yourself,
the stronger the feelings grow
There is something inside
that is trying to come out
Give it some room; talk to it
Ask yourself questions about it

There is nothing to be afraid of,
for it is only you needing to be comforted
You needing to be taken care of,
You needing some space for yourself
Waiting for answers to come to you
Do you not know that you must seek the answers?
There is help available, but there is also work to be done

You have not found your passion
You circle around it like a hawk, but you have not landed
Your interests flit from one thing to another
Landing briefly like a butterfly and flying off again
The way home is not always a clear path
Often, it is littered with remnants
from the past that hold us up
Sometimes we are distracted
by shiny objects that attract our attention

When the "Meaning of Life"
question crops up, pay attention
For you are sending a signal to yourself,
a message that needs to be heard
Give yourself permission to listen
Let down the barriers that prevent you from hearing
Surrender, if only for a minute, to the need inside
Experience the profound and exquisite transformation
Look in the spaces between the pages of your life
For that is where the lost may be found
and the true meaning of your life is hidden

Clear your mind of clutter
That you may hear yourself think
The time is near
The seconds are ticking away
Doing what is right can cause havoc
Lessons learned and shared, lessons repeated
All have meaning

Remember your walks to school
The time spent playing with daisies
Each memory in your life holds something dear
They all contribute to the total you

Yet some memories cause us pain
Sending us to the depths of despair
Gripping us as if in a vice
The low times can be hard
We separate ourselves
from the world for a time
We gain insight

Our empathy for others grows
as we begin to understand ourselves
Reaching out comes from reaching in

The story goes that
an old man needed food for his children
Fearing that he might not live to see them grown,
he began setting something aside

He worked industriously only to find
that what he gave of himself was
more important than what came from him
His life experiences made him wise
Through pain and suffering he learned compassion
He could love others unconditionally,
because he had learned to love himself

We live on the edge of forever
Our minds racing from yesterday
to today to tomorrow
Wanting what is best for those we love
Praying that the world will hold itself together
The mind is always working
Looking for ways to survive

Necessary as this is, it is not enough
For it is only one piece of the whole
We also need our lighter side
Our laughter and joy, our love of humanity

The key to it all is balance
The key to balance is
being in touch with yourself
Letting go of the past
Hearing what your body and spirit are saying
Appreciating the gifts each day brings
The future is something to think about
but not to live for
The present is where it is at
Easier to say than do,
but worthwhile nonetheless

They only come to those who are ready
Those who are open; those who are aware
They choose deliberately,
because they don't want to be discounted
For some, it is a great effort, for others not
They have no ulterior motives, only to make contact

In times past, people had visions
and were more easily able to connect
They crossed over and back more freely
Today, few are at that level
Our understanding of the other side is limited,
no travel guides available

Response to visions is mixed,
both personally and socially
World opinion matters not, but it is there
For some it is a comfort, a validation of life beyond
For others it is disquieting
Raising questions they do not wish to answer
Dreams have been an avenue
of communication for thousands of years
The meanings of which have been hotly debated

Cast not your duties to the wind,
lest they be carried away forever
Rather, accept what is given to you
Wait not for a signal from the heavens
before you believe

Crossing over is a simple task, like taking a breath
Getting ready to take that breath can be more difficult
For most, it is a process started
internally long before the day
You walk where you have not
walked before, yet it feels familiar

The process can be long or short, fast or slow
Loved ones can be part of it, if they choose
Once there, the process continues
Preparing us for other experiences

Revelations are few
But wisdom, oh wisdom,
is attainable by all and of far more value
For what we know enhances where we go
The sweet breath of spring speaks of birth
The hot winds of summer speak of growth
Maturity is the password of autumn as slumber is of winter
All can happen in a moment or in a thousand years

The process is the same for individuals and for societies
One person at a time, one step at a time
All leading to the cumulative growth of mankind
We expand in different directions,
some outwardly, some inwardly
Outward growth connects us with this world
Inward growth connects us with another world
Sometimes we want it
Sometimes we don't

Spirit growth allows us glimpses
It can connect to those we love
or to new experiences
It opens our pathways
and gives us tools to find our way
The glimpses are cherished gifts to us
from those on the other side
They happen when we are ready
and when they are ready
A meeting of the minds so to speak
Happening when we least expect it

Your guides are many,
some with names some not
Names are of importance to you not us
What you do with names matters not
Worry not, for the words you hear
are not false

The chatter in your head
that surrounds them cannot be helped
For in this connection between two worlds,
the line is not always clear
The meanings of the words cannot be predicted
for they fall upon different ears

Concentration is sometimes an issue
A wandering mind has
little space for thoughts
An open mind is like a vessel
through which much can flow
Thoughts, feelings and impressions
can easily be passed
The space is the thing – neither here nor there
Open to communication and aware enough
that it does not slide through

Fret not over details as concept is the key
Worry not about tense
There will always be matters to speak of
and ideas to be exchanged

The worlds are different
Separated by the concept of life
Propped up by the fear of death
They seem to exist separately when,
in fact, they are intertwined
Kept separate to avoid confusion
Giving every soul its own opportunity

Souls standing back, lending a hand when needed,
a driving force when necessary
A whispering breeze, not a conquering hero
A bird on your shoulder,
not an elephant on your chest
Tapping, not pounding
Sometimes helpful, sometimes not
We cannot force, only suggest
Voices from the other side
offering assistance
One point of input among many
Sometimes heard, sometimes not
but always there

Look at your whole life, not just a part of it
Start at the top and work your way down
Look at what makes you happy
But also, at the sadness
It is stuck in little pouches
here and there

Shed the anger that seethes through your body
For it weighs you down more than you know
Begin in small ways to rid your life
of unnecessary things

Crack the veneer that keeps you separate from others
Be willing to give more of you and of your Self
For when you do, many things will open to you

Our first duty is to take care of ourselves
That means nurturing ourselves,
our relationships, our dreams
Watching carefully
how we connect with others
Keeping the walls we build to a minimum
Realizing that our way of relating to the world
may be different than those around us

Before you were here,
your connection to the Universe was strong
Pray for that connection to be strengthened
as it is the key to everything

The place where you are is the place where you are
Start from there, going neither backwards
nor looking ahead
Pray for the strength of spirit
that will lead you where you need to go
Pray for the drive and determination to get you there
Pray also for the stamina to proceed
for the way may not be smooth

The hole you feel inside can only be filled by you
There is no magic potion or any person that can fill it
When it is full, you will be done
It is like a deep well
whose level rises and falls with the rain
But whose source is the reason for its existence

Rely not on others to fill the hole for you
Rather, realize that you are the source
That through your actions and connections
Through your connection to yourself
and to the Universe
Your source will expand

You have the key
It is all there
Sometimes patience runs thin as you search
Sometimes desperation seeps in
Remember the importance of the journey
For all the lessons we learn along the way
lead us in the right direction

Peg Roberts   **168**

The commitment is not to others but to yourself
Make the commitment and stick to it
Your soul and your spirit are part of you
and you are part of them
How could such a combination
be anything but wonderful?

Healing

The crossing of one's fingers does not
solve problems nor does the wringing of hands
Marching stalwartly across a field does not help,
if you are looking for an ant
As you run your hands across the body,
listen for a click
Watch for a bump, be aware of any change
in the smooth pattern flow

We are there to intensify the energy; to create openings
Just when you think there is nothing there
A little voice may whisper in your ear

As you progress, our presence
may grow stronger, our voices louder
The idea is to work together for the best outcome
Long distance healing is our specialty
We will go wherever you send us
The energy is growing thicker

One act of healing will save a thousand souls
Use your power wisely
Reveal it only to those who believe
A time will come when the responsibility
will be solely yours
Prepare for it now

Develop your abilities to the *n*th degree
Share your success with others
The sun is setting on the old ways
The new light on the horizon
is for the benefit of all
Cherish the new-found wealth

Healing has nothing to do with time, but with intent
The body will replenish itself when it can
A wounded spirit is sometimes harder to heal
The clash between body and soul disrupts the energy field
Gaping holes can appear
The body's ley lines become displaced
The life source begins to seep away

Restoring the energy fields
is like repairing a leak in a dam
It soothes the soul as well as the body
In ancient times, a well was a precious thing,
for it was the source of all life
So, too, with the energy,
for it comes from the source of all life
The price one pays to heal is the
time one gives to others

In return, one receives untold peace
Place your hand upon the rail
and begin to climb the stairs
An angel will guide you
Don't you think that it's time to get started?
Your wishes can come true
You need only make it happen

There are many things upon your plate
Some large, some small
Yet all are of equal importance.
for they hinge upon each other
Create for yourself an open space
in which to lay out everything
Examine each item carefully
Turn it over in your hand to see all sides

Toss aside those items that are of no worth,
as dealing with them uses valuable time
Also, set aside those things
about which you can do nothing
From the rest, choose two
upon which to concentrate
Chief among them is health

Allow blockages to melt away
Let in the light of health
Give it room to grow
Why do you not take the proper care?
Do you not know that you are worthy?

Clamber over self-imposed barriers
Look at them
See them for what they are
Once they are removed,
motivation will no longer be an issue

Peace &
Surrender

Ask a question of yourself and the answer will come
The fogginess inside your head will lift
as clouds from a mountain top
Your whole being will work
to find the answer, for it has no choice

The answer may be in the trickle
of a brook or the buzz of a bee
You may hear it in the passing comment
of a friend or the dialogue of a play
You may read it in a magazine
or in the writings of a child

But have no fear, the answers will come,
if you are open to them
For are we not vessels of our God?
Do we not have access to our own Truths?

Elusive as they may seem to be
They are there waiting for you
Your access to knowledge and truth
is limited only by the questions you ask
Ask wisely or with abandon
It matters only that you ask and
that you be willing to hear the answers

Be a child of the Universe
Hear what is being said to you
Struggle not to find answers
Let them come

A short meditation may free up more information
than hours of research in a library
For a life's directions are not prepackaged
The harder you look, the more obscure the signs

The solution is to surrender to yourself
Listen to the messages that are inscribed on your soul
In them are your lost peace and tranquility,
your insight and inspiration
Look inward to truly see and hear with your heart
that you may be fulfilled

Contrary to popular belief, the end is not always last
Tread softly lest you interrupt the story
My word is not the word of law but of spirit
Comfort thyself with its tone

Where there is injustice, let justice prevail
Address each issue in its own time
Wince not in pain
Rather, ride upon its crest to study its depth,
for within it lies peace

A peace born of anguish and hurt
A physical peace and a spiritual peace
Each born of its own type of suffering

Get to know your pain intimately
That you will learn to comfort yourself
For from all things is there benefit
From all things do we gain wisdom
Keep thyself present in all that you do

Go for the long ball
The thread of life
was never meant to be short
Come into my house
and see what has transpired
The candles are still lit,
but there is a new energy
Feel it in your heart and in your soul
Look through my eyes at the vast expanse
Let the vibrant colors surround you

In this world, we have many destinies
We choose or allow ourselves
to choose some
Others choose us
Despite our meanderings,
we get where we have to go

Destinations can be elusive
Funny things happen along the way
We get caught up in life's little mysteries
Chasing rainbows and catching butterflies
Keeping the future at bay
Giving to others of our gifts

For you, the future is at hand
Knocking at your door
Let it in lest it passes away
Cherish all that awaits you

You have much to give
But also, much to receive
Let your cup overflow
with the grace that is yours

Release the demons in your soul
For you no longer need them
Erase the pain of the past
For it only weighs you down

Come forth from the cave of doubt
and bask in the sunshine of contentment
See yourself in the new light,
surrounded by love
Walk where there are no shadows
Listen to the song your heart sings
Its melody is your strength

As you walk among the children,
reach out to their souls
For they are part of you
and you are part of them
Peace will come in a thousand ways
Serenity will settle down upon you
Tranquility will run through your veins
and you will feel at home

Come unto me that I may shelter you under my wing
Lay your head on my breast that you may
hear the heartbeat of the Universe
For until you have surrendered,
there will be no peace

The waiting and the watching will continue
Indecision will plague you
Discontent will be your companion
You will flounder about with no anchor
The quest for perfection will continue
The path you follow can lead anywhere
You need not search for answers,
as they are already there
You need only find ways to get to them

A trumpeter swan's great beauty
is not apparent at birth
Thorns do not spoil the beauty of a rose
Lightning refreshes the summer air
Start with what you have
and make it work for you
This is not a competition
There is no race

Giving up is a slow and gentle process
You give up by giving in – letting go
Stop fighting

Giving up is not a defeat, but a victory
An acknowledgement of the real you
An ascent to the top of the mountain
The feeling of which
is impossible to describe
You do not surrender yourself,
but surrender to yourself
Establishing a oneness, a connection

Be not distracted by the trappings of the world,
for they pull you in other directions
Wash your hands of falseness
Beware of truth tellers with no heart
For the truth need not be blasted
into the ears of others

The real truths come gently
and of their own accord
They slip into us unnoticed
They whisper to us when we least expect it
We sit at truth's feet and truth sits at ours
The body and the mind can come together as one
with the soul – listening and letting go
Not of ourselves
but of our expectations of ourselves
Surrender gives freedom to our souls

*I*n all things be clear
Answers are not always obvious
It is a matter of timing
Visions of the future,
stories of the past may intertwine
Sharing their messages

Unseen personages create,
Spirit guides project
In the ether world, no one is idle
There is no interest in lying on clouds
or floating through the air

We press forward
Always aware
Always watching the flow of life
Having no goals of our own
We support others in creating their lives
Comfort is of no concern to us
though we try to bring it to others
Rarely seen by some,
commonly seen by others
We are always there believing,
accepting and encouraging

Courageous acts unfold
Monumental decisions are made
Lives are saved
Food is shared and homes are built

We share our energy, our wisdom
and our process when asked
We connect with those who are ready
We watch over our families

The power of inspiration
cannot be taken lightly
Spiritual sensitivity cannot be dismissed
Seeing beyond the physical plane
is not impossible,
for we are all one in spirit

Keeping in touch with one's Self
is not only possible but necessary
The Spirit touches us all
We are guided by it
and we guide by it
Coming as we are from a place of peace

Humanity

The new world order seems rather like the old
Boundaries change, new governments
appear but the struggle goes on
The foul puss of old hatreds bubbles
to the surface, spawning tragedies and war
Will we never learn the lessons?
Does each generation have to start from scratch?
Is there no way to profit from the mistakes of the past?

Oppressed people yearn for freedom
to do and say what they please
Like children eager to grow up
and be on their own
But with freedom comes responsibility
When no one else can tell you what to do,
you must look to yourself
Ask yourself what freedom means
How best it can be used

To speak out?
To rail against an enemy?
To slander?
To commit atrocities
in the name of freedom or God?
To seek a new horizon?
To work with others?
To let go of hatred?

The world is small,
a molecule in the universe
Kingdoms, nations, republics
States, cities, towns, and villages
Homes, families, and individuals
Flesh, blood and bones with spirits and souls
All created from the same energy

Judge not by the color of our skin
For the energy does not come in colors
Judge not the Gods we worship
For the energy is universal
and encompasses us all

A single thread connects us
like a giant string of beads
Our destinies entwined
Great and small, sick and well, rich and poor
Brought together by acts of kindness
Torn asunder by violence and hate
But always connected by the thread
For if the thread were to break,
there would be no order in the Universe

There are those things that touch us all
The innocence of youth
The smell of fresh mown hay
The gentleness of a touch, the midnight sky
Behold them all with dignity,
for they represent purity
Untarnished by greed or power,
without motives

Drink in the serenity they provide
Their worth is not valued in dollars and cents
But in their gentleness
as it settles upon the Earth

What touches you?
The rainbow after a spring storm?
Puppies rolling in the grass?
A father playing with his son?

Make your list and hang it for all to see
That they may make their own lists
There is enough beauty to go around
For if there were a list for every wall,
a pleasant scene in every mind
Perhaps the world heart would flutter
The voice of man would be a little less gruff
and humanity would take one small step
in the right direction

There are many possibilities
There are no revelations to be told,
only paths to be walked
The plan is always in the making
The joy or sorrow of the day
comes from the actions of those involved

Nation to nation or person to person,
the principle is the same
Let no man raise a finger
without realizing the consequences
Let no nation think that its power
is enough to conquer the world
For within power lies destruction

The seeds of creation spring from the loin
The sustenance of civilization comes from the heart
For only through love can mankind thrive
Narrow mindedness sets love aside
Intolerance puts conditions on it
Racism declares some unworthy of it
Hatred obliterates it

With love in our hearts, and a willingness
to become whole, the picture changes
Differences shrink from monoliths to pebbles
Understanding grows from a
single spark to a strong flame
The need for power and money lessens
when the focus is on people instead of things

Intent is of utmost importance
Where you want to go
determines where you go
What you want to be
determines what you become
How you want to do these things
determines how they are accomplished

The paths are many
We all choose our own
The journeys are the stories of our lives
Each of us a potential
candle of hope for humanity
Each with the capability of
contributing to the greater good

Each new century, year, day and minute
is a clean slate upon which we write
The decision is ours
It is up to us
We create the future
through our thoughts and actions
The future is in our hands

A company of soldiers sets off across
the desert with one thing in mind
To end a conflict forever
In truth, the conflict never ends
For the world has never
come to terms with itself

Prejudice, intolerance, greed
and a need for power continue
The soul of man is wounded
The heart of the world has missed a beat
Humanity has suffered a blow

On the surface, a country, a way of life has been attacked
Streams, which once ran clear, may seem a little clouded
A breeze that ruffles your hair may feel different
A plane in the sky has a different connotation
The perception of the world has changed
What does one do – pray, get angry,
give blood, become depressed?

In times of great peril,
we must look to ourselves
For the road to change starts with us
We are all guardians of the world
The shepherds who will lead those who follow
Our ways will become their ways

If we hug and love our children
They will hug and love theirs
If we walk freely among all peoples
It will not go unnoticed
If we embrace our differences
instead of condemning them
It will draw us closer
If we talk with each other,
understanding will grow

For in the end, all the praying, crying and
mourning will not change the world,
if we are not willing to change
Military solutions will change the
face of the earth, but not the fabric of humanity

When we pray for others, we must also pray for ourselves
That we may let go of intolerance and prejudice
That we can see clearly what is truly important in our lives
That the love we have for others can be given
without restrictions or conditions
That we can forgive others for
what they have done to us or those around us
That we recognize the connection
between us and the rest of humanity

For we are all one people
All grown in the womb of a woman
All born in innocence
Our spirits and souls
all part of the same Universe

The borders of countries were created by man
The love of the Universe has no boundaries
We must not let the borders become barriers
that prevent us from connecting with each other
Setting us against each other
Creating mayhem
Let us reach out instead,
both physically and spiritually
to envelope the world with love

A Handful of Reflections

The process of discovery can be long
Don't try to figure out
what you're supposed to do
Following the right path doesn't mean
that there is only one path

Opportunities are everywhere
Some we do not see
Some do not appeal to us
but they are there

Drawing up a life plan requires a lot of strength
Bouncing from pillar to post does not
A perfect moment can occur
at any time or any place
A child in the cradle seems
soft and vulnerable
but maybe as tough as nails

Weep not for the baby
who has passed into adulthood
For he has stepped over the threshold

*W*alk as one with us
Oh, ye who walk the Earth
Worry not, for we will show you the way
Let yourself be loved

→ *T*he time has come
to let your heart direct you
The message is clear
Confusion reigns supreme in places
where the heart is not heard
The comings and goings of
everyday life cannot be changed
The shift has to be more subtle

In all things, be appropriate
➤ Outcomes don't come until later
In all things be clear
For the design is laid out before us
➤ In times of need, there will be answers
→ In times of stress, there will be support

*B*ehold, the answers that we seek are before us
For reasons unknown, they come to us
Sometimes in a flash
Sometimes disguised as other questions
Being open to everything clears the channels
and allows the light to enter and expand
Your light is special and has made a permanent
mark on the world

*K*eep my spirit close to your heart
In thy wisdom, keep thyself open
This joy has no boundaries
For the lessons to be learned are many
Walk slowly that you may take it all in
Be patient, for revelations come in due time
The beauty of light is in the glowing
The beauty of life is in the being

Serving two masters is difficult
Agitation causes conflict
Still, nothing changes
The promise of a new beginning
The long wait for yet another sunrise
When shall it end?

The indiscretions of diet play havoc
When the leaves fall off the trees, drink tea
Keep starches to a minimum
and eat more greens
The heart will benefit from fish
Cook it well
Keep it simple

The kidneys need to be flushed
Drink fluids that are clear, without extras
The body benefits from a variety of foods
In the evening, place cucumbers
on your face for 15 minutes
Let the juice do its work
A hot water and oatmeal soak may
help the hands, followed by aloe

*I*n the shadows of our minds, doubts abound
Left from times when we were not sure
Sometimes they gnaw at us, putting us in spaces
where we do not need to be
The power to withdraw
from those spaces is within us
Remembering to draw upon it
is another matter

We get caught up in the old ways
Barriers separate us from ourselves
They rise and fall
Keeping us in and others out
When threatened, we retreat
When safe, we come out
The way to overcome is through the heart
Place yourself in the hands of the one
who can guide you
The rest will follow

*T*he process is different for everyone
Keep the energy going through practice
Awaken your spirit to the tunes
that are being sung

The response we have to the deeds
of others is a reflection of us
The source of our consternation
or pleasure in what others do is inside us
Our compassion responds
to the compassion of others
Instincts, too, play an important role

The content of the book comes
naturally once the plot is in place
The hard work is laying out the plan
Thoughts turned into words on paper,
then turned into deeds
One thing at a time, one step at a time

Tie up loose ends
lest they drag upon the ground
Hold close the sheaves of paper
lest they fly away
Make use of your connections
The prize can be won by everyone

What is obvious depends on the seer
Coming upon an accident, a physician would
check a person's physical condition
A minister would be concerned for the
person's spiritual well-being
Each focused on what was obvious

The plain truth hovers around
the edges of your existence
Invite it in
The course of history will not be
altered by it, for it is simple
Plain truths seep into your soul
They speak softly, but their impact is great

Know ye this – that the greatest truths
are not of this world
Embedded as they are in the Universe
Small specks in the cosmos
They are the underpinnings of us all

Receive into your heart this knowledge
that you may be aware
Be open to stray thoughts that feel good
Let the spirit of your soul guide you

*T*he space between here and there is not large
It consists only of a dot and a speck
Getting from here to there is another matter
Geese fly across the pond
to a new nesting site
Frogs lay their eggs
All are looking at new beginnings
It is not planned, but simply a part of the plan
You got yourself this far
Have faith that you will make it all the way

*S*hallow minds do not wander far
for they search not for the truth
A question, once answered, is no longer a question
Once the people of Kobertam were in despair
They could not move for their lives had no meaning
Time after time, they were beckoned to but few responded

God whispered in the ear of one woman
She rose up and moved about
without knowing why
"There is something I must do,
but I know not what," she said
So, too, do we go through our lives searching

$\mathcal{A}$ pale feather floats down
from the sky and lands in a soft place
A moonbeam shines through
a window on a sleeping babe
Mother Earth stretches
as she tries to keep herself awake

$\mathcal{W}$onderful light, marvelous light,
that attracts all to it
Play your song for me
Come alive in me,
that I may hear your words
Remain in me that I may learn your ways
Prepare me for what lies ahead
As I slumber, plant seeds in my mind
that will challenge me to think
Give me the courage to cast off doubt
and be open to new ideas

The art of photography has limitations
The art of life has none
Combining the two
can have interesting results
Beneath a blanket of snow life stirs,
even though it can't be seen
So too does life stir in other dimensions
A flick here, a flame there, a flash of sunlight

One soul or many making their presence known
A rare gift, given to us in the best of situations
Brought about by strong connections
Seen by some as a mistake
As an apparition by others

Within a matter of minutes, things happen
A quiet lake becomes angry
Swarms of locust cover a field
An ice cube becomes a puddle
The question becomes
not whether to act, but when

If an ant and a bee were to wrestle,
what would be the purpose?
In an angry mob, there are leaders,
who know why they are there
They incite, but have no control

A coach works with a team
so that each person knows their job
In a perfect world,
we would have teams and not mobs

About the Author

Peg Roberts was born and raised in Massachusetts. Her love of the ocean led her to live and write in seaside communities in both Florida and Massachusetts. She has three wonderful children who have blessed her with six grandchildren. In addition to writing, Peg also practices Jin Shin Jyutsu and Reiki to help herself and others stay healthy.

Five Women Publishing was established in memory of five women in my family who were excellent writers. None of them sought to be published and none would have thought their writing was worthy of being in print.

In Memory of
Edith Courtis Johnson
Edie Johnson Porter
Evelyne Johnson O'Neil
Ruth Johnson Girard
Judy Girard Hordon

It is our hope that honoring these five women prompts other women to value their own talent and encourages them to share their writing gifts with the world.

Ordering Information

New books coming soon!

Dear Reader,

If you liked this book, I would greatly appreciate you writing me a review on any online book site.

I look forward to sharing more ideas and insights with you in future books.

Thank you, I really appreciate your help.

Regards,

Peg Roberts

Five Women Publishing
P.O. Box 1423
Newburyport, Massachusetts 01950
info@fivewomenpublishing.com
www.PegRobertsAuthor.com
Peg@PegRobertsAuthor.com

For information about special discounts for bulk purchases, please email Five Women Publishing at:

info@fivewomenpublishing.com.